Martin Solutions Group
ISBN:

Interior Design and Layout by Taccara Martin

Cover Design by Taccara Martin

THE HEALING JOURNEY

Kenyon and Taccara Martin

Authors' Note

Dear Reader,

Welcome to "The Healing Journey: The Soul-Ties Detox." This book represents a decade-long evolution in our understanding and approach to the concept of soul-ties, a journey that has been both enlightening and transformative for us.

When we first released our work as "Journey to Freedom: The Soul-Ties Detox" ten years ago, our primary goal was to dispel the myth of soul-ties and challenge the popular teachings that often mislead many on their paths to healing. We dedicated a significant portion of our introduction to debunking these misconceptions, aiming to set the record straight.

Over the years, we've spent countless hours discussing, teaching, and refining our approach. Kenyon and I have been deeply committed to helping people break free from the chains of unhealthy relationships and erroneous beliefs. However, we now believe it's time to shift our focus from debunking myths to guiding you on your personal journey of healing.

In this rebranded edition, we are excited to present "The Healing Journey." The term "Soul-Ties Detox" now carries a double meaning: detoxing from unhealthy relationships and detoxing from outdated ideas of soul-ties. Our goal is to redefine soul-ties based on sound psychological principles and God's intelligent design, while also giving you the language to describe the invisible hurts and wounds that you've been

Authors' Note Cont.

carrying.

We invite you to step back from preconceived notions and allow this book to guide you. Whether you are seeking freedom from past relationships or a deeper understanding of your emotional and spiritual well-being, we hope this book serves as a comprehensive guide on your path to healing.

Thank you for joining us on this journey. We are honored to walk alongside you as you embark on this transformative process.

With gratitude,

Kenyon and Taccara Martin

Table of Contents

How to Use This Book

The Soul-Ties Detox is a 40-day program that was designed with your healing in mind. This will probably be one of the most challenging processes you have ever gone through because it will require you to defy everything your heart wants you to do. However, if you truly want the process to work, it will require a level of commitment and self-discipline that will seem impossible.

As much as toxic relationships or toxic partners hurt us, it's amazing how much their presence and promise of change eliminates the pain you feel almost instantly. Everything inside of you will want to err on the side of hope. However, if we're honest, hope is what has you in this place right now. The hope that they will change back to the person you fell in love with. The hope that their behavior is just a phase and will get better with time. The hope that, if you can just be better for them, they will become better to you. So while this process will make you feel as if you are abandoning them and yourself, you will actually be abandoning the mentalities and habits that have contributed to your pain, even if it means abandoning hope—in the way you knew it, at least.

This program is divided into six weeks. Each week has a deliberate goal of helping you break the "ties" that oppress you. It begins with an educational foundation so that you can learn what soul-ties are and how they affect you. Then it will transition into weekly activities that will help you "walk out" your healing journey.

In the end, you will have reclaimed your story and developed a persistent practice of cleansing and protecting your personal and emotional space.

You likely purchased this book because you are looking to "get over" them and move on. We understand that you are desperately seeking a way to make the pain stop, but it will take time. So the first challenge you will face will be to not rush through this book or program. Take this one day and one week at a time, and try not to read ahead or become preoccupied by what happens next week. Intentionally focus on the week that you are in so that you can be present and wholly absorbed by each week's activities. It's like long math; once you learn it completely, you can take shortcuts later.

Your sense of safety and security has been lost, but you didn't end up here overnight. It took time to build a relationship that you trusted and felt safe in. Then that trust was broken. What happened next only seemed sudden because of the stun you felt after what you thought you had was pulled from under you. Whether a relationship lasted three months or three years, you'll learn in this book that so much more than your recent relationship contributed to where you are today. So give yourself grace and time here. Resist the temptation to hurry yourself, resist the temptation to hurry us as your coaches, and resist the temptation to hurry God.

Within the book are six chapters that we'll refer to as phases. Each phase is a part of a week, and each week has a designated number (e.g. week two, phase three). You'll know that you've come to the end of a designated week when you read or hear "That's the End of Week __." Don't go any further. Meditate, review, and complete the exercises as thoroughly as possible.

Weeks are based on seven calendar days; this way you can begin on any day of the week. If you start your week on a Thursday, then that week of progress should end on the following Wednesday. Then you would begin your new week the next day (Thursday). Due to the seven-day week, we urge you to take your sabbath rests. Mental and emotional rests will be necessary during this difficult time. Taking a rest does not mean that you relax your guard, lower your standards, or stop progress. It means that you take a day or two for rest, meditation, or prayer. It's your "me time" as well as your "me and God time."

Be sure to complete all the assignments. Each assignment has a purpose. If a question or something does not apply to you, then fill in the answer with "N/A" (Not Applicable). This helps you practice the habit of completion. We want you to walk away from this process with no unanswered questions.

Track Your Progress

This program and its assignments will require you to write . . . a lot. So we advise you to either purchase a journal or keep an electronic journal for your journey. It may not be apparent when you begin, but doing this will let you see and refer back to your progress, even when you don't feel like you're progressing. In the end, your writing will be a powerful testimony for you to treasure and share. After you've completed the program, we suggest continuing to use journaling as a way to document your continued growth.

Don't Take This Journey Alone

We don't want you to take this journey alone. You didn't get here alone, so it's important that you don't try to exist and exit alone. You will need a Personal Support System (PSS). The PSS is a trusted person in your corner who will provide you with emotional support during down days or when you need to vent. They will also help push you through your exercises and keep you accountable. Listen, we all fall, but we don't have to fail. Your PSS catches you when you fall, and that support helps to keep you from failing.

When choosing a PSS, ask someone who is fully invested in your recovery and supportive of your success. It's important to choose a non-judgemental person that will keep you accountable and doesn't mind pushing you. They have to be comfortable with becoming lovingly unpleasant when you need that "coach" in your ear.

Additionally, make sure that you ask someone who you will listen to. This can't be someone that you find easy to brush off. You'll need a PSS who you respect and who you'll respond to out of that respect. Someone who is worthy of being a part of your testimony.

Finally, if your PSS is not a direct relative, we strongly recommend that your PSS be of the same gender. This is for your emotional safety. Emotional pain makes it easy to become intimately distracted. You will be exposing some of the most intimate parts of you, and if you attempt to go through this process with someone of the opposite sex, it can inadvertently cause this person to become the next unintended object of your affection. This will stagnate or stop your progress.

In layman's terms, you do not want to be catching feelings while those same feelings are hurt. You'll end up getting hurt again or hurting someone else.

Once you choose a PSS, have them read The PSS Support Request found in the back of the book.

After your journey, if you find yourself running into others who have gone through what you've been through, consider becoming their PSS. You will now have an ability to relate and to empathize with their struggle. Additionally, you will have a testimony that shows them that healing is possible.

Your initial experience with the Soul-Ties Detox will likely not be your last. Life happens, and people will continue to cross boundaries that hurt you. Use this program as many times as you need to for new situations and people. Once the detox is understood and becomes a habit, it will no longer take weeks to process.

We recommend that you use the Soul-Ties Detox as a once-a-year cleansing, preferably during the beginning of the year. The new year gives you a traditional time stamp on letting go of the past and moving into the future. Many church communities are already participating in a corporate fast at the beginning of the year, and this program can be complementary to that fast. The Soul-Ties Detox is an actively powerful supplement to your periods of prayer and emotional cleansing. This can be your new yearly routine for release, forgiveness, and moving forward.

There are small group discussion questions listed at the end of each chapter. Those questions are for church and support group moderators. As an individual, you do not have to complete those questions, but you are welcome to complete them in your journal. The more questions you answer the better. You never know, you may be leading a group later yourself.

Small Groups

The Soul-Ties Detox program is ideal for church small groups and individual support groups. Since this program calls for a PSS, small groups and support groups provide the best kind of support. There is an inherent sense of understanding when everyone involved is going through the same thing. Groups can provide accountability, empathy, personal help, and encouragement that may not be found in family or friends.

The Soul-Ties Detox is good for the following types of small groups:

- Singles
- Pre-marital
- Newly Wed
- Husband-Only or Wife-Only
- Post-Divorce

Small Group Leaders —————————————

When you are a leader, your group may see you not only as the facilitator, but they may also look to you for guidance. You will be a prayer warrior, cheerleader, and a trusted confidant. Do not take this responsibility lightly, but do not wear it heavily either. Know your limitations.

Remember that you are not alone. While you are the facilitator and guide, you don't have to shoulder any responsibility that you are not prepared for. The book does the teaching, the people do the work, the Holy Spirit helps you lead, and God provides whatever is lacking. You are not personally responsible for anyone's success or failure. Be sure that you are engaged with a pastor or church leader to lean on when you encounter situations beyond your ability to help.

As a leader, we recommend that you have gone through the program at least one time first. While it is not an absolute requirement, having previously participated in your own journey eases the initial "blow" of the process and prepares you to lead from a place of empathy rather than an emotionally desperate place. When you go through the process first, you can navigate discussions better and prepare the group on what to expect the following week. Your personal testimony will provide tremendous encouragement.

Each chapter ends in small group discussion questions. These questions are icebreakers for group conversation. As a leader, please feel free to add more questions to further the conversation.

A Practical Guide for Leading Small Groups

Making the small group safe is a priority. Here are a few ground rules to help achieve that goal:

Be Non-Judgmental – We all hurt in various places. Do not judge a person by their hurt or by how they arrived at that hurt. Support them.

Be Accountable and Hold Each Other Accountable – This program best works through consistency, dependability, and discipline. Accountability helps you to help each other stay strengthened.

Be Confidential – Nothing should leave your meetings to be shared, gossiped about, or used to shame or deliberately hurt another. Couples are to make sure it's okay to share about their marriage. Their marriage is not just their story, it belongs to them both.

Be Respectful – Be aware of sensitivities. Do not probe or question to satisfy personal curiosity. Do not cut others off while sharing. Be polite. Be empathetic and responsible with the hearts surrounding you.

Be Supportive – To be supportive is to be a servant. You do not need to have the answers as much as you simply need to be present with an individual that needs you.

Each participant in the small group will go through the program weekly as we described earlier. The group itself, and a partner within the group, will serve as a PSS, so try to have even numbers as much as possible. The group as a whole will go through the Soul-Ties Detox simultaneously, but each member will have to go through their own individual process

15

away from the group.

The nature of this program makes it necessary for your small group or support group to be safe and free from judgement or condemnation. Confidentiality and empathy are paramount factors of the detox group. Wounds can be uncovered, secrets may be told, and members will find themselves vulnerable in ways that even they are unaware of. Create an environment where everything that is shared in the group stays in the group.

The individual PSS's are also bound by this same secrecy. They should not share anything with the group (or anyone else) without the permission of their partner. If there is a specific concern about what has been shared privately, that concern must first be shared with the PSS partner. Then the PSS must ask permission to share with the leader of the group only. If that permission is not granted, the PSS should simply encourage their partner to share with the leader themselves.

If concerns involve abuse, molestation, rape, stalking, intimidation, or anything illegal or life-threatening, consider encouraging that individual to seek the help of professionals or law enforcement authorities. Professionals include medical practitioners, clinical counselors, faith-based coaches, or anyone of an official capacity that can provide protection, guidance, or service. Prior to reporting, a PSS should express their concern over the situation to their partner.

We highly recommend that small groups and support groups are divided by gender. It is a human tendency for someone to seek comfort in another human being when healing from hurt or trauma. For many, pain is quieted by romance and affection. Being wanted, desired, validated, embraced, or even sexually soothed serve as a self-medicated distraction from their pain. So to support an emotionally safe environment, we recommend the small groups or support groups be gender-specific.

Marriage Small Groups

Sometimes a marriage small group will adopt the Soul-Ties Detox program to help an individual get through something that is challenging their marriage. That may be anyone from a toxic parent, family member, friend, ex-partner, or an outside party where there was an affair. If this is the case, we recommend that spouses be separated by gender as well. Spouses may need their vulnerabilities protected, and sometimes that means from each other. There may be instances where a spouse cannot take knowing that their husband or wife has unresolved issues. Due to these personal vulnerabilities, spouse-only groups can help keep marriages safe and reduce the harboring bitterness during and after the program.

In general, we assume that marriage small groups and support groups have a goal to support marriages. However, we want to reiterate to participating spouses that their partners come first. Confidentiality within the marital relationship is extremely important. Discretion in speaking about your spouse is urged. Each husband and wife must be very sensitive about what is shared within any group setting. Always consider your spouse and their feelings.

Now, with all this considered, let's get started.

WEEK ONE

INTRODUCTION

The Spirit of the Sovereign Lord is on me, because the Lord has anointed me to proclaim good news to the poor. He has sent me to bind up the brokenhearted, to proclaim freedom for the captives and release from darkness for the prisoners, 2 to proclaim the year of the Lord's favor and the day of vengeance of our God, to comfort all who mourn, 3 and provide for those who grieve in Zion—to bestow on them a crown of beauty instead of ashes, the oil of joy instead of mourning, and a garment of praise instead of a spirit of despair. They will be called oaks of righteousness, a planting of the Lord for the display of his splendor. **Is. 61:1-3 (NIV)**

Introduction

There I was, lying in bed, balled up in the fetal position, and crying my eyeballs out. He had hurt me to my core, and yet I couldn't stop "accidentally" calling him. I couldn't stop replaying all the lies, all the cheating, and all the times he'd hurt me over and over in my head. I couldn't stop trying to figure out what I had done to deserve a pain like this or what I could have done differently to prevent this undoing of me.

I couldn't sleep. I couldn't stop tossing and turning. And on the days that I'd almost succeeded in "forgetting" him, my phone would ring and I'd quietly hope it was him. I couldn't stop wanting him to finally see me and love me. But the more I tried to get him to love me, the more rejected I felt. The more I tried to seek closure from our break-up, the more broken I became.

My testimony didn't begin with the heartbreak from the man described above. It began with the rejection of my biological father. Being born to a man who considered their child a mistake has a way of hindering someone in romantic relationships. Everything I grew to know about love was of a works-based mentality that forced me to believe that, if I did (insert any and everything I could imagine to get his attention), then my father would see me and love me. And guess what? The more I tried to get him to love me, the more rejected I felt. Every relationship I had, including the one with my faith and God, was poisoned by the idea that I wasn't good enough. So, I had to work harder.

I grew up in church, but even there I felt like I had to maintain a certain approval rating to be accepted. What they did not approve of was counseling or anything that required me to seek help outside of the Bible or them. Counseling and therapy were for people who didn't know God. So when I struggled with brokenness and defeat, and prayer didn't feel like it was working, I'd begun to think I either wasn't good enough or that I wasn't doing enough. I attended all the revivals, altar calls, and healing services that I could, but I was still suffering. Not to say that miracles don't happen or that others can't be delivered through these venues, but that wasn't my experience.

Finally, in a moment of desperation, I cried out to God and began to seek true change. Something clicked, and to this day, I can't tell you what it was; I just knew that this time I was done. Being done to me meant that I didn't care about the other women. I no longer cared to uncover what was true versus what was false in his tangled web of lies. I stopped torturing myself trying to find answers in his behavior. I just wanted to be free. This is the moment God was waiting for. It was almost as if God grabbed my hand and said, "Okay. Now let's get to work." It has been more than 14 years since those desperate moments, and I am happy to say I am still free and still unbound.

In all fairness, it's important to point out that, when I had initially begun to seek healing, I wasn't being totally honest with God. I would go up for prayer and seek healing for the man I was with but not for me. I wanted God to stop my hurting by forcing this man to treat me right so that we could live happily ever after. However, that's not how healing works and, thankfully, that's not how God works either.

You are about to go through a process that God used to show me myself—not just my reflection in the mirror, but the condition of my heart. I didn't just end up in toxic relationships, I was shaped in them. It wasn't enough to identify and remove myself from those who hurt me in relationships. I had to understand why I desired love from people who would never love me the way I deserved. So, I detoxed using the same process that you are starting today.

While my husband and I are shamelessly in love with God, this process will incorporate a combination of a biblical focus, practical guidance, and our personal gifts of wisdom earned from our testimony. Your journey will encompass both psychology as well as theology, where you will learn how God's spiritual design for you also supports his biological and chemical design. We'll identify the "whys" and the "hows" of our humanity to develop a healing process that will speak to the whole person. Once you can understand this, you will be better equipped to go on a journey toward freedom.

Why 40-Days

The number 40 is a significant biblical number. It identifies the beginning of a period, journey, or transition. The beginning of that period, day one, is marked as a start of something. It is a place of potential, a place of patience, and a place of perseverance. The last day of this period will be a place of deliverance.

There are two significant times that Christ had a 40-day experience. The first time was at the very beginning of his ministry. After baptism, Christ spent 40 days in the wilderness. In this place, he fasted, his humanity was tested, and in the end he prevailed. When Christ came out of his 40-day journey, he showed up with power, surety, and direction. He was prepared for his purpose.

Christ's other transformational 40-day period was after his resurrection. During the 40 days following his resurrection, Christ continued to teach and empower those that followed him. At the end of those 40 days, they would come to anticipate his promise of power in the coming of the Holy Spirit (Acts 1:3).

Spiritually speaking, we believe that the next 40 days will be a pivotal time for your deliverance, transformation, and validation. We want you to intertwine your faith with this process. Let the practical steps you take meet the promise of the power at the end of your journey.

Scientifically speaking, there is no set designated time to break or build connections, habits, or behaviors. While there are various theories out there, what we've found is that when it comes to breaking habits or behaviors, consistency over a period of time is key. However, from experience with previous clients, we've seen that approximately 40 days of focused, intentional commitment to this process does induce transformation.

What is truly miraculous about this process is that God gave both Kenyon and me these same instructions during different times in our lives. It wasn't until we started our ministry together and people started coming to us for this same type of help that we realized we had gone through the exact same process individually, only years apart! This is how we know that this program is God-ordained and designed. I firmly believe that God inspired us to frame the spiritual, structural, and practical process in such a way that it will move you confidently towards deliverance without question.

This program will cause you to develop a new way of thinking about the friends, loved ones, and even family members that have hurt you. However, don't begin this process if you are not ready to be honest with God and yourself. Don't begin this process if you are still holding on to hope that the person or people who have hurt you will eventually come to their senses and do right by you. It's not to say that they won't, but you cannot predicate your healing on their actions. This is for you and you alone.

"But I have prayed for you . . . that your faith may not fail. And when you have turned back, strengthen your brothers." **Luke 22:32 (NIV)**

Those who have successfully completed the Soul-Ties Detox program often "sealed their testimony" by doing something that signified a renewed spirit and a new life. Some changed their phone number. Others changed their address. I moved clear across the country. The one thing that we ask you to do when you have finished this journey is to seal it with service. Simply help someone else. Both Kenyon and I have lost a lot. Both of us have been failures. Both of us have been crushed by relationships . . . broken. But we were not being broken solely for our benefit. We were broken for you.

When they asked Jesus about a blind man, and if it was because he or his parents had sinned that had caused his condition, Jesus said, "Neither this man, nor his parents sinned, but this happened so that the works of God might be displayed in him." John 9:3 (NIV)

We were healed to glorify Christ and to share our testimony with you. Once you have completed this part of your journey, our prayer is that you are just as changed. We pray that distrust becomes vigilance. We pray that anxiety becomes peace of mind, that anger becomes forgiveness, that depression becomes rejuvenation, and you'll receive beauty (redemption) instead of ashes (lamentation).

Then, when you have overcome, you will be able to share your testimony with another. We have included a coupon code in the back of this book for you to share with someone after you have completed your journey. This will be your way of paying healing forward so your brokenness can be used to bless another. This is how the Gospel works.

We are so excited to meet you on the other side of this journey. We're praying for your strength through this entire process that your faith will not fail.

PREPARE FOR DETOX

You are still in week one. Please continue on to the next phase.

WEEK ONE

PHASE ZERO

EDUCATION

Trust in the Lord completely, and do not rely on your own opinions. With all your heart rely on him to guide you, and he will lead you in every decision you make. Become intimate with him in whatever you do, and he will lead you wherever you go. Don't think for a moment that you know it all, for wisdom comes when you adore him with undivided devotion and avoid everything that's wrong. Then you will find the healing refreshment your body and spirit long for. **Prov 3:5-8 (TPT)**

Phase Zero: Education

If you're anything like most of the people we've supported on their healing journey, you are probably stuck somewhere between "I can't do this anymore" and "Why can't I let them go?" You volley between these emotions because not only do you love them, but often you don't understand or have the words to describe what is happening to you. You literally "go with the flow" of your feelings until it makes you feel like you're going insane. Our goal with this phase is to give language to your experiences and to help you honor your feelings while putting them in their proper place.

As humans, we have been taught to respond to and cope with our experiences by feeling with our emotions, thinking with our head, and doing through action. While feelings, thoughts, and actions are all ways in which we respond to most anything, only one can be trusted to lead in your decision-making, especially during times of brokenness. When you are feeling hurt, confused, distraught, angry, or broken, you cannot rely on your feelings. Like a broken leg, you cannot stand on or depend on something that is broken. So while it's important to honor your humanity and your feelings in this moment, you'll need to resist your natural inclination to make decisions based on your feelings.

We understand how hard that seems, since your feelings are what brought you here. We're not saying to ignore your feelings. What we are saying is that you cannot depend on how you feel to guide you while you're in this program. The anxiety, the sadness, the hope, the "what ifs," or the "why me," or the "how did I let this happen" are all feelings that, if allowed to dominate your thoughts, will guide your actions. Mentally obsessing over situations tends to lead to decisions or actions that you will immediately regret, which usually leads to more hurt feelings or more negative thoughts. And the cycle begins again.

We don't want you going through that. So, take a moment and imagine three light switches. The first switch is your head switch, the second switch represents your hands, and the last is your heart. The head switch represents thought, the hands switch represents action, and the heart switch represents your feelings. These are what we call your leader switches. Whichever switch is on is the one that leads the others in operation. Right now your heart switch is on, which means your emotions are leading your thoughts and your actions.

In continuing with this imaginative exercise, we want you to intentionally decide what will lead you going forward. So imagine yourself turning your heart switch off. See that in your mind. Close your eyes if you have to. You will still feel, but you now understand that you do not have to follow how you feel. Now say this out loud to yourself: "It's time to change what is leading me, so I'm turning my heart switch off." Repeat this exercise anytime you begin to feel overwhelmed.

You're not done. If your emotions are not leading you, then we need to turn on the switch that should be leading you right now. This is your head switch. We need you thinking in a way that processes information through your rational mind, not your feelings. Your feelings may react, but they cannot be allowed to initiate action.

In continuing with this same exercise, find your head switch on the wall of your mind. Imagine looking at it and seeing that it is off. Your head has been working, it just has not been leading. Now imagine turning your head switch on. See that in your mind. Close your eyes if you have to.

This is you exercising your personal will and discipline. You will experience emotional surges where your heart will want to take over. That's normal when your heart has been leading you for so long. Only now, you will have to stay in tune with yourself so that you can immediately sense when your heart is leading, and then turn your head switch back on. As you will yourself through this part of the process, be intentionally conscious of where you're going and what you're doing.

Let's Begin.

———————————— ℰℰ ————————————

"Getting wisdom is the wisest thing you can do! And whatever else you do, develop good judgment." **Prov 4:7 (NLT)**

Phase zero is like ground zero. This is the place where the calamity and catastrophe originated, whether you saw it coming or not. And before you can begin to heal properly, we have to begin cleaning up the emotional rubble and debris. This starts with the way you think.

We'll start by dispelling a few myths that have often misled people in their healing journey. These myths will keep you tied to toxic people and toxic relationships. There's a difference between the bondage of circumstance and the bondage of thought that keeps you bound in that circumstance. These myths that we will address can keep you passively hoping for change and stop you from actively participating in your deliverance. If you don't actively participate in your own rescue, you will stay bound and likely repeat the same mistakes over and over again.

Myth #1: Time Heals All Wounds

The Truth: Time alone does not heal all wounds. Time with intentional effort of rescue, recovery, and rehabilitation results in deliverance that brings healing.

Has anyone ever told you:
- Give it time?
- Get over it?
- This too shall pass?
- Wait on God?

If yes, then be honest. Have any of these statements ever really helped you, without any effort on your part? We want to be careful. This isn't a knock against God. What we are saying is that God would not have you sitting around aimlessly waiting for help, change, or healing. Time alone cannot induce true change without accompanying action.

Imagine a scar from a deep cut or burn. Of course it healed over time, but not time alone. The wound had to be cleaned, disinfected, and maybe even stitched. Then it was bandaged and isolated for a period of time. Wounds left open and untreated put your entire body at risk for unnecessary infection and pain. So, just like your physical wounds, your emotional wounds must be cleaned, treated, and then isolated for a period of time. The entire process works together with time in order to facilitate healing.

Most cases of emotional hurt are a result of deep wounds below the surface with fresh injuries compounded on top. If you find that you keep ending back up in the same or similar toxic relationships, it's possible that much of the hurt you're experiencing is likely due to unresolved issues of the past—issues you assumed were resolved simply because time had passed.

Some issues originate from as far back as childhood and adolescence. Others may stem from young adulthood. Some issues have been perpetuated in adulthood. But if you take a close look at some of the events in your past, you may find patterns repeated in your present. Unhealed wounds or past issues will always resurface and either consciously or subconsciously affect today's decisions and relationships.

James 4:7 suggests that there are two things that must take place in order to remove the enemy. The first is submitting to God, the second is resisting the enemy. Submitting to God precedes everything that leads to deliverance and healing. That submission comes by relationship, understanding, and demonstrated trust in him.

The second thing you must do is resist. Resist the enemy in whichever form it may come. The enemy to your healing can be people, places, or anything that is able to hinder or block your progress. Resisting is more than turning away or simply trying to mentally block the things out that can hurt you. It's about confronting what's in front of you, identifying why it's a hazard to your healing, and then intentionally labeling it as an enemy.

Assigning this label to your enemies immediately strips them of their power and allows you to make more informed choices with your "head switch" instead of your heart or emotions. But the operative action in all this is to confront. You can't afford to wait for them to go away. The enemy will always seek to capitalize on what you do not confront.

"

The Enemy Will Always Seek to Capitalize on What You Do Not Confront.

Myth #2: Name It and Claim It

Unfortunately, you cannot speak your way out of what you willfully walked into. Yelling and decreeing at the enemy in the name of Jesus can be a form of catharsis or emotional relief, but the problem is that you are still the same person that made the decisions that have brought you here. And while emotional relief may feel good, and even be necessary, it does not address the need for mental and emotional behavior shifts within you.

We're not here to bash your theology. The altar or altar-call experience is not bad. The altar only becomes bad when we misrepresent it as the final place of our healing. Lay your burdens down there. Cry there if you must. But when you get up, commit to changing your mind, habits, and behavior so you don't end up there again for the same hurt. The altar is where your healing begins.

In John 5:6 when Jesus asked the disabled man if he wanted to be healed, many could read that and assume that Jesus was being funny or even cruel. The man was there at the water where healing was taking place. Of course he wanted to be healed! But the fact that Jesus had to ask him suggested that something in his mind was crippling his ability to walk more than his legs were.

When you read the scripture further (John 5:7), you'll notice that the man never even answered Jesus or stated that he wanted to be healed. He merely responded out of the mentality that he had grown accustomed to in his sickness. Even though he appeared to want healing, even though he was at the waters where the healing took place, he had not prepared his mind to sustain him in that healing. Allowing you to name and claim a new life, a new heart, or a new experience without a new you would be unloving of God as your Father. God does not perform passive rescues. He will always provide a way for you to get to your destination, but you have to be willing to crawl, walk, or run to it.

Let's take a look at the Israelites when they were delivered from the hands of Pharaoh. During their exodus journey, they were told they would be delivered during the last night of the last plague. They had to carry out very specific instructions: sacrifice a lamb; prepare dinner; eat standing up; be ready to leave—fast. And did you hear about the part where they had to cross through a sea? Nothing about that deliverance was passive.

The children of Israel partnered with God for their rescue, and this is what you must do as well. Trust God and partner with Him through this process. God is waiting for you to participate in your rescue, and we have instructions that will get you to your "promised land." Get up, get dressed, pack, and be ready to hike out of this place of your suffering. After the wilderness of walking out this program, you will be a new you.

The Wilderness

The wilderness is that bitter place between you finally moving away from the toxic relationship you knew you needed to escape and the promise of wholeness. And even though the promise of wholeness is enticing, the journey there is uncomfortable and lonely. When the children of Israel were in their wilderness, they complained about the discomfort of their freedom and reminisced about the pleasures of captivity. They even considered going back. It wasn't because they missed the pain, but because they missed the familiarity and predictability of their prison.

During this journey, you're going to find yourself in your feelings quite a bit. You will miss them. You will find yourself frustrated and even complaining about the pain of this process. We understand. The wilderness has a way of making you believe that those toxic connections made you feel better than the loneliness you feel right now. But that will be your heart switch where your emotions are leading. When those feelings show up, turn your heart switch off, turn your head switch on, and keep going forward.

It took the children of Israel 40 years to reach their promised land. And because some still carried a toxic mentality, parts of them had to die, while the others had to be rebuilt in order to become someone new. So we will spend the next 40 days together creating an environment that allows parts of you to die (metaphorically speaking) so that the core of you can be rebuilt to become someone new.

The Power of Repentance

Now that you are choosing to move forward, your choices belong to you. When someone has hurt you, it is understandably difficult to admit how you participated in your own pain. It's hard to honestly acknowledge the times you had the opportunity to choose a different direction but didn't. We are not victim-blaming here. And we never want to suggest that someone chooses abuse or to be physically or psychologically tormented. What we are asking you to do is take an honest look at some of the situations that have resulted in emotional hurt and ask yourself, "Did I have an opportunity to avoid this by making different choices?" If the answer is "yes," then it's important to acknowledge those choices, take accountability, and commit to going in a different direction.

Repentance simply means that you are changing your mind about how you've carried on and committing to choosing a different direction.

You Were Not Made to Fall but You Were Designed to Survive The Break

Here's the good news. Just because you have failed or have been failed does not mean that you are a failure. Just because you have been broken to a point that feels beyond repair does not mean that you are irreparable. You are lovable and worthy of love, even if someone else did not have the capacity to love you right.

God loves you. And while in a perfect world you'd never fall, He knows that this world is not perfect. He has made you in such a way that, even though it's not his will that you fall, he has designed you to withstand the impact of your fall. You can heal from this. But if you allow yourself to feel hopeless in your brokenness, you will continue to remain paralyzed by it. So, as you continue in this journey, be encouraged. Be strengthened. Be changed.

You are still in week one. Please continue on to the next phase.

"

You Were Not Made to Fall But You Were Designed to Survive The Break.

Notes

PHASE ONE

WHAT IS A SOUL-TIE?

14 So then, we must cling in faith to all we know to be true. For we have a magnificent King-Priest, Jesus Christ, the Son of God, who rose into the heavenly realm for us, and now sympathizes with us in our frailty. 15 **He understands humanity,** for as a man, our magnificent King-Priest was tempted in every way just as we are, and conquered sin. 16 So now we draw near freely and boldly to where grace is enthroned, to receive mercy's kiss and discover the grace we urgently need to strengthen us in our time of weakness. **Heb 4:14-16 (TPT)**

Phase One: What Is A Soul-Tie?

This is going to blow you away. Can you imagine that there was a time in American history where cigarettes weren't just popular, they were even prescribed by real doctors? Today they're basically outlawed, but back then, cigarettes weren't just the rage, they were the norm. Not fully understanding something but wanting to capitalize on it anyway is a dangerous recipe. That's what happened with cigarettes. They were popularized and capitalized on because opportunity far outweighed the unseen or ignored dangers.

We are not saying that soul-ties as an ideology is dangerous like cigarettes, but we cannot deny the popularity of the term. We cannot deny how many have capitalized upon that popularity. As a result, we cannot deny that there is an existing danger in how "soul-ties" is being used.

The unfortunate problem with today's use of soul-ties is that the desperation for answers make those who need answers vulnerable to almost any answer. It's an issue that is hardly fact checked or studied because those in need are blinded by their existing pain. In other words, people in need are vulnerable to anything that feels like help.

That's why soul-ties is such a sensitive subject. It's not just because of the popularity; it's also because it is attached to meaning. That meaning brings hope to the hurting, which is great. It's just that there are so many meanings out there that soul-ties may be the name of the pain, but the method of addressing them can be almost anything.

We never want to invalidate anyone's pain, and we won't invalidate what you name that pain, but in order to get real results, you need to know what soul-ties really are and what they are not. You need to know how they work and how to break them. You need to know the truth.

What Soul-Ties Are Not

The history of soul-ties is a convoluted mess that seems to have popped up out of nowhere. We've not been able to pinpoint a date of "discovery" or who coined the term, but we learned that it became a relevant term in the mid to late 20th century. Soul-ties grew popular in Charismatic Christian circles, but it isn't exclusive to Christianity. The most common version of the ideology can be associated with Christianity, Christian mysticism, and the New Age movement.

Because we are Christian coaches, we are only interested in the current popularized Christian version of soul-ties. The struggle is that it shares so many similarities with non-Christian versions that it is hard to separate the different kinds. We've distilled all of the commonalities and explanations for soul-ties into the general definitions below. Some will be familiar, some will be new, but all of it is connected.

Definitions

● **Soul-Tie** - A soul-tie is a bonding, tying, connecting, chaining, or knitting of the actual souls of two individuals. This used to be explained as happening only within sexual relationships. However, in recent times, soul-ties have been defined to include all intimate relationships. This includes romantic covenant relationships (i.e. marriages), non-sexual relationships (i.e. friends or family), and non-covenant sexual relationships (i.e. adultery, affairs). When the soul-tied relationship is broken, the two literal souls that are tied together are fractured.

● **Soul-Fractures** - The broken souls that come as a result of a break-up between two people who are soul-tied in a relationship are called soul-fractures. While you don't hear soul-fractures mentioned by those who popularized soul-ties, soul-fractures are heavily inferred due to the literal nature of a soul-tie. Soul-fractures, whether named or not, is the reason for personal brokenness when a break-up or abandonment occurs. The result of a soul-fracture or broken soul are soul-fragments.

● **Soul-Fragments** - The pieces of a soul that are broken off after a soul-fracture are called soul-fragments. This is also never stated directly but is strongly inferred due to how they explain soul-ties as literal souls. After brokenness, it's hard to let go. This is because the broken pieces of a soul are taken from the original person and attached to the other person in the relationship. So a person loses "themselves," quite literally, while maintaining pieces of that other person as a continued bond.

Short Definition Recap

An intimate relationship that literally glues or ties two souls together is called soul-ties. When that intimate relationship is broken, both souls are fractured, which creates soul-fractures. These fractured pieces of soul break off into fragments, called soul-fragments. Each person in the relationship loses parts of their own soul-fragments and keeps parts of the other person's soul-fragments. A person with repeated broken relationships collects other people's soul-fragments while losing more of their own.

All of this is supposed to explain the emotional turmoil of break-ups, divorces, abandonments, and abuse. It's supposed to explain why you feel personally broken and why you can't let go. The swapping and collecting of actual souls are supposed to be the explanation for why you feel like you feel right now. Really.

Now, if you've heard of soul-ties before, you probably haven't heard all of this. You've likely only heard the most popular rendition of soul-ties. That's because the popular part is what gets your attention, especially in Christian circles. Regardless of what they leave out, their explanation presupposes the nature of the soul as something that can be connected to, tied to, broken off, lost, and received by someone else.

Are you starting to see the problem here? We got questions,

and you should have questions too!

Questions like:
- How does that actually work?
- Are souls physical?
- Can the soul actually be tied, fractured, or fragmented?
- How many fragments make a whole soul?
- How many fragments can be lost before your entire soul is gone?
- How does that work when someone close to you dies?
- Does a piece of your soul go with the dead?
- Does a piece of their soul stay with you?
- How many deaths or break-ups can you take before you're not you?
- How can you tell when you're no longer you anymore?
- Where are tied, fractured, or fragmented souls in the Bible?

If we are honest with ourselves and apply a little critical thinking, the questions are endless. These are all valid questions. As Christian coaches, the most valid question for us is the last one: "Where are tied, fractured, or fragmented souls in the Bible?"

Christian popularists have developed a sort of biblical argument for soul-ties. We are going to explore the main scriptures they use. Then we'll show why these scriptures don't work. This next part is a bit lengthy, but be patient. Due diligence is necessary.

"Do your best to present yourself to God as one approved, a worker who does not need to be ashamed and who correctly handles the word of truth."
2 Timothy 2:15 (NIV)

Context, Meaning and Translation

Here's the primary scripture they use to argue that soul-ties are biblical.

"And it came to pass, when he had made an end of speaking unto Saul, that the soul of Jonathan was knit with the soul of David, and Jonathan loved him as his own soul." 1 Samuel 18:1 (KJV)

Now that certainly sounds like there are two souls being knitted or tied to each other. But are they really? Is this scripture being read in context? Context is found by reading the complete thought and not just one verse. Reading the complete thought in context gives us what the author intentionally wanted to say to his or her audience. Let's look at the scripture in context and with meaning.

18 And it came to pass, when he [David] had made an end of speaking unto Saul, that the soul of Jonathan was knit with the soul of David, and Jonathan loved him [David] as his own soul.
2 And Saul took him [David] that day and would let him go no more home to his father's house.
3 Then Jonathan and David made a covenant, because he loved him as his own soul.

4 And Jonathan stripped himself of the robe that was upon him, and gave it to David, and his garments, even to his sword, and to his bow, and to his girdle.

5 And David went out whithersoever Saul sent him and behaved himself wisely: and Saul set him over the men of war, and he was accepted in the sight of all the people, and also in the sight of Saul's servants.

6 And it came to pass as they came, when David was returned from the slaughter of the Philistine, that the women came out of all cities of Israel, singing and dancing, to meet king Saul, with tabrets, with joy, and with instruments of musick.

7 And the women answered one another as they played, and said, Saul hath slain his thousands, and David his ten thousands.

8 And Saul was very wroth, and the saying displeased him; and he said, They have ascribed unto David ten thousands, and to me they have ascribed but thousands: and what can he have more but the kingdom?

9 And Saul eyed David from that day and forward.

1 Samuel 18:1-9 (KJV)

This passage is actually about Saul and how he went from hot to cold on David. First it shows how Saul accepted and loved David—so much so that Saul never let David go home because he took David in as a son. Saul loved him like a son, and Jonathan loved David like himself, even closer than a brother. David was being adopted into Saul's royal family.

We needed to see Jonathan's high level of love in order to see the contrast of Saul's level of hate. To Saul, David wouldn't be anything without him. No one would know who David was without Saul treating him as part of the family. So, when David gained fame over Saul, Saul took it personally.

That's the gist of the meaning of the passage. Now, let's look at a couple of words in the native Hebrew language. The first word is "knit." Does "knit" mean something physical in this passage? The Hebrew word translated as "knit" is the word "qasar." Qasar means to bind or tie, but when it's used regarding a relationship between two people, it means a deep love and shared covenant. When Jonathan and David are "qasar," they agree together, are in one accord, and are in league with each other. That's why Saul began to see their brotherhood as a plot against him.

"That all of you have conspired [qasar] against me, and there is none that sheweth me that my son [Jonathan] hath made a league with the son of Jesse [David]..." 1 Samuel 22:8 (KJV)

The Hebrew word used earlier for "knit" is the same word Saul used here, but it is translated as "conspire." "Knit" and "conspire" are two words that describe a deep bond. Jonathan loved David and was bound (knit) to David in mind, heart, and life. Saul witnessed that bond (knit) and later saw that bond (knit) as a conspiracy against him. "Knit" is not literal.

Next, let's look at the word "soul." The Hebrew word translated as "soul" is the word "nepes." Nepes means life, mind, heart, and breath. This is a description of ways Jonathan was bound to David. It was a close bond in mind, heart, and life. The New Testament would call this equally yoked. Saul lost that kind of closeness to both of them, so he saw their heartfelt bond as a conspiracy.

Imagine that someone said that you stole their heart. Does that mean that you took the organ out of their chest without consent? No. It's a metaphor to describe that without effort you gained their innermost affections. It's poetic, which is common in biblical literature.

The passage of 1 Samuel 18 isn't Jonathan considering a piece of himself and David that can be physically tied, broken, lost, or fragmented. Jonathan is considering a bond of their hearts, minds, and a sense of life. In a very Hebrew way, this is a metaphor of David being fully accepted and deeply loved by Jonathan.

Let's reread the scripture with this in mind.

"1 And it came to pass, when he [David] had made an end of speaking unto Saul, that the life/heart of Jonathan was bonded with the life/heart of David, and Jonathan loved him [David] as his own life." 1 Samuel 18:1 (KJV)

Let's look at a different translation:

After David had finished talking with Saul, he met Jonathan, the king's son. There was an immediate bond between them, for Jonathan loved David. 2 From that day on Saul kept David with him and wouldn't let him return home. 3 And Jonathan made a solemn pact with David, because he loved him as he loved himself. 1 Samuel 18:1-3 (NLT)

What About The New Testament? ————————

When the Bible introduces concepts that have the potential to affect us in a personal and spiritual way, the Bible doesn't leave us hanging. It introduces the issue, demonstrates the issue, and then gives the resolution of that issue. The best examples are specific sins like lust, fornication, laziness, or drunkenness.

When it comes to soul-ties, there is no biblical introduction, address, inference, or resolution at all. If losing pieces of your soul was truly in the Bible, and if it was really a problem, then there should be scripture to address and resolve it. The Bible has plenty of bad relationships as opportunities for literal souls to be tied. Think of Abram and Hagar, Jacob and Leah, Samson and Delilah, Amnon and Tamar . . . and that's just the Old Testament.

Jesus was concerned for more than just the law; he was concerned for the heart and spirit of a person. Jesus was well aware of what we call the Old Testament. If souls could be literally tied and broken, then not only would Jesus know about it, but he'd be concerned about it.

Jesus had two distinct opportunities to address the existence of the literal form of soul-ties:

Exhibit A: The Woman at the Well
The first opportunity for Jesus, was the Samaritan woman at the well (John 4:4-26). When he met her, Jesus pointed out that she had five husbands. He also pointed out that she had a man in her home that was not her husband. Jesus exposed

this woman's intimate life to her while speaking of spiritual things. Yet he didn't say anything about tied or broken souls. Jesus was in the business of deliverance, healing, teaching, and even exorcisms, yet he had nothing to say about the potential loss or fragmenting of a woman's soul from multiple intimate relationships.

Exhibit B: The Woman Caught in the Act of Adultery
Another case is in John 8:1-11. Here we're introduced to a woman caught in the act of adultery. This woman was dragged out into the street due to sexual sin. Out of all of the occasions of intimacy and brokenness in the Bible, this one was perfect for some sort of soul break. Sex, infidelity, adultery . . . this is the perfect time for Jesus to address, heal, and cast out some literal soul-ties, right? You would think so, but he doesn't. He addresses those who judged her, forgave her, and instructed her in her sin.

Both of the aforementioned situations were environments conducive to this false definition of soul-ties. Deliverance is not just a part of Jesus's ministry. Deliverance is Jesus's ministry. Jesus never mentions, infers, addresses, heals, helps with, or delivers anyone from any soul-ties. Why? Because this kind of soul-ties does not exist.

Let us say this loud for the folks in the back. We don't care who your favorite pastor, preacher, prophet, or evangelist is, if they promote soul-ties as a literal bonding of physical souls, they're wrong. Misrepresenting soul-ties as a theological doctrine, especially with no biblical support, borders on heretical.

More importantly for our focus, using scripture to gain people's trust in bad doctrine means that, at some point, that doctrine will show it doesn't work. That's dangerous to the faith of people we're trying to help. It will lead hurt people into emotional catastrophe and personal crisis of faith.

What Makes The Soul-Ties Detox Different?——————

That is a fantastic question. As pastoral counselors and agents of healing, part of our goal is to help give language and meaning to your emotions and experiences when you don't have them. When we initially started helping people do the work of healing, we vehemently rejected the idea of calling what they were dealing with "soul-ties." What we eventually noticed was that we were spending so much time trying to get people to remove the term "soul-ties" from their vocabulary that we were not able to focus on the actual work of healing.

When people don't have a name or the language to describe what they are dealing with, they can develop a sense of hopelessness because they feel like they are stuck dealing with something that no one understands. We never want to invalidate someone's pain, so we adopted the term "soul-ties." When someone is able to name their pain, it confirms that their suffering is real and gives them hope that something can be done about it. The pain of a broken heart is a broken soul-tie. Now, our goal is to retrain people to understand what hope looks like by showing them how their pain actually works.

The second reason why we adopted the term "soul-ties" is because we literally do see God in soul-ties, and it's actually not mysterious or confusing at all. There is biblical context for why broken hearts affect us this way. We must acknowledge our human nature in a biblical way that honors how God made us. Properly defined soul-ties biblically fits God's design and purpose for human relationship.

The "soul" in soul-ties, when properly used, demonstrates our natural affinity for relationships as God has designed us. Remember, the biblical definition of "soul" is "nepes." It was used to identify great love, commitment, and loyalty. It is a term that speaks of deep, intimate, and affectionate mental and emotional impact. The voluntary dedication of the heart, the mind, and the breath is a practice of devotion. When used properly, "soul-tie" is the perfect term for the description of intimate relationships that God has designed us for.

Our Definition of Soul-Ties

Soul-ties are strong physical, mental, and emotional bonds that exist within intimate relationships. These bonds produce feelings of connectedness and attachment in our relationships, creating a strong sense of care and concern. When soul-ties are formed, they forge environments for physical connection that also create biological changes. Although soul-ties are commonly used to describe intimate connections in romantic relationships, they also include non-romantic connections within family, friendships, and acquaintances.

When soul-ties (intimate bonds) are broken or are not properly formed, it can cause mental and emotional distress, as well as trigger physical and physiological responses in the body.

Soul-ties are intimate relationship bonds not made to be broken. When soul-ties are broken, it breaks you.

God's Role in Soul-Ties

Relationships and the soul-ties that bind them have purpose. There's purpose in their function and in their representation. Both are set up by the purpose giver: God. His design for how we operate in relationships is directly connected to how he desires intimate relationships to reflect him.

"Then God said, 'Let us make mankind in our image, in our likeness, so that they may rule over the fish in the sea and the birds in the sky, over the livestock and all the wild animals,[a] and over all the creatures that move along the ground.'" **Genesis 1:26 (NIV)**

God created humanity in His image as a reflection of Him. Your reflection in a mirror may look like you, but on the other side of what you see is actually glass and aluminum. The same goes for God's image. God is a spirit and we are his reflection made of flesh and blood. Humans were designed to look like God in function and representation in a physical way on Earth.

God's omnipotence (power) is reflected in the human function of earthly dominion. God's omniscience (knowledge) is reflected in our learning and discovering this earthly dominion and its inhabitants. God's omnipresence (everywhere-ness) is reflected in our spreading out upon this Earth through the physical act of reproduction. Government, communities, friendships, and families are all a part of that reflective purpose. Absolutely none of that can be done without relationships.

Relationships aren't just a function to achieve God's purpose of earthly dominion. Relationships in and of themselves are also a reflection of God's image. God is one (Deuteronomy 6:4). God is infinitely and eternally perfect oneness. God is relationship. God the Father, God the Son, and God the Holy Spirit is one perfect, intimate relationship.

To be made in the image of the Spirit of God is to be made for relationship and oneness physically. Every relationship we form in life sets the stage for the next one. The first intimate relationship we have is usually with our parents and our family. How we form bonds and attachments in our familial relationships helps us better prepare for deeper connections in marital intimacy and oneness. Intimate oneness is so much a part of who we are, it was woven into the human exchange of attachment.

——————————————— ℒℒ ———————————————

> "That is why a man leaves his father and mother and is united to his wife, and they become one flesh." **Genesis 2:24 (NIV)**

That statement indicates that:

1. Intimate parental relationships must be broken from in order to accommodate a new type of oneness.
2. The actual anatomy of marriage is defined by two people becoming one in an intimate and committed relationship.
3. In the Bible, the relationship between children and parents and the relationship between husband and wife are the intimate building blocks of communities and nations.

We seek and desire relationships because it is a part of our purpose. The beauty of intimacy is found in the reflection of affection, closeness, and connection. This purpose is completed within the family (i.e. parents and children, and husband to wives). A nation is but multiple communities of families acting, behaving, and identifying as one. This is the intimate function and reflection of dominion.

Adam and Eve

The Lord God said, "It is not good for the man to be alone. I will make a helper suitable for him." 19 Now the Lord God had formed out of the ground all the wild animals and all the birds in the sky. He brought them to the man to see what he would name them; and whatever the man called each living creature, that was its name. 20 So the man gave names to all the livestock, the birds in the sky and all the wild animals.

But for Adam no suitable helper was found. 21 So the Lord God caused the man to fall into a deep sleep; and while he was sleeping, he took one of the man's ribs and then closed up the place with flesh. 22 Then the Lord God made a woman from the rib he had taken out of the man, and he brought her to the man.
Genesis 2:18-22 (NIV)

Let's look at this closely. God was already aware that Adam would not be able to populate the Earth, have dominion, and reflect Him by himself. Adam needed someone to do that with. But there was a process that God needed to follow with Adam. The first step was for Adam to learn what God already knew. So, God gave Adam the task of naming the animals. As Adam observed these animals, he discovered that every animal had another of its own kind to help it meet its God-given purpose. Adam learned that he was the only of his kind; he was alone.

That loneliness is such an important principle. God was there, yet God knew Adam was alone. Adam didn't know he was alone until he discovered that there was nothing else like him that he could relate to. There was nothing that he could mentally, emotionally, or physically have a relationship with. This is a clear response to the difference between a physical human and a spiritual God. God made us as physical beings on purpose. As a result, there are needs that we have that only relationships with another human can fulfill.

The second part of this process was for God to meet Adam's need. And God met Adam's need from inside of Adam. Why? Because that's the closest He would get to having someone like Adam for relationship. This is so critical to understand. Adam's body was altered for the purpose of preparing him for relationship. It's not just a rib. Adam's blood, tissue, nerves . . . his anatomy was directly affected by the process of bringing him into relationship.

Experiencing intimate relationships is far more than just wanting someone to hang with or sleep next to. It's a physical, emotional, biochemical, neurological, habitual bond. This is what we mean when we speak of soul-ties. Intimate relationships, be they family, friends, or romantic connections, change you—as if your "rib" was being adjusted. So when that intimate bond is broken, you are actually broken.

This is Your Brain On Drugs

Do you remember the 80's commercial that used an egg to demonstrate the effects of drug addiction on your brain? The man in the commercial cracked the egg into a hot skillet and the skillet fried the egg. The message was that drugs fry your brain.

The example was extreme, but it made a good point. Our brains are chemically and physically altered by foreign or unfamiliar substances. Love does a number on your brain in the same way drugs do. Love is the process of unfamiliar people gaining intimate access to us in a way that alters our mental, emotional, and physiological functions and bonds us to a person. Just like the rib from Adam, this is God's plan.

During times of emotional bliss, like falling in love, your brain is baptized in natural drugs that your body produces. This seductive cocktail of neurotransmitters like adrenaline, dopamine, and serotonin literally changes the way that you think, feel, and behave.

Adrenaline makes your heart race and gives you sweaty palms when you're nervous. The blood pumps with liquid excitement, anxiety, and even a little fear generated by attraction. This is when your heart literally skips a beat. But your heart didn't skip a beat because it was telling you that he or she was "the one." It was a chemical response to an attraction and the anticipation of connection.

Dopamine gives the sensation of being rewarded. It's the good feeling of intangible pleasure when that person is nearby. There's something about being with them, talking to them, and engaging with them that makes you want more. You want to call them, text them, or run to see them every time you think of them. Being with them feels good, and dopamine causes you to constantly look for them when they are not around. Even when you sleep, you're captivated by them, and it feels good.

Serotonin keeps you happy. It really improves your overall mood by blocking sadness. Nothing can get to you or get you down while you're serotonin-happy. Your overall good mood and sunny disposition directly correlates to thoughts of your new love interest.

When studied, researchers even found that couples who were newly in love exhibited symptoms similar to people with OCD (Obsessive Compulsive Disorder). They had anxious thoughts (obsessions) that cause uncontrollable, repetitive behaviors (compulsions). This shows up in sudden unexpected phone calls or texts throughout the day or even checking your phone repeatedly to see if they've called or texted.

These biochemical and physical changes create environments for bonding to someone and building attachments. They also support the development of deeper bonds as you spend more time together. This is a process of oneness.

Welcome to Love . . . Shaken, Not Stirred.

As you begin to attach to someone, two additional chemicals join the party in your body: oxytocin and vasopressin.

Oxytocin is a powerful agent with the specific purpose of bonding. This chemical has a stronger and more intense effect when intimate touching is involved—especially with sex and after an orgasm. Oxytocin is found in men and women, but it's stronger in women. That's because it is the same chemical that causes mothers to bond with their nursing babies.

This chemical alone is the main reason why we find more women than men struggling with broken soul-ties. It's not a fractured soul, it's a broken emotional and physical bond that was designed to never be broken. Women who continue to suffer from this type of brokenness will find it increasingly hard to bond to someone else. When this type of brokenness occurs repeatedly, it can inhibit the body's ability to produce oxytocin.

Vasopressin is the biochemical that facilitates bonding and attachment within men. Released after sex and during the journey of bonding, vasopressin is what increases possessiveness in men. Men respond to bonding by becoming more protective, territorial, and jealous. Vasopressin intensifies their instinct to secure their significant other.

The Hangover: The Key to Understanding Your Emotional Pain

We've given you a small peek into the biology and emotional psychology of intimate relationships. Both love and emotional attachments are parts of our genetic design. Everything about how you feel right now is due to God's desire for you to feel the same type of love and connectedness to another the way He feels connected to us. By looking at the scientific and the practical aspects of how you were created, it becomes easier to understand why you feel and act the way that you do in relationships. Whether they are romantic or non-romantic relationships, this divine and purposeful act of human bonding is what we call soul-ties.

Soul-ties are God's handiwork and craftsmanship. We're designed so that our chemicals work in concert to change us in preparation for oneness. Even our brain neurologically adapts to accommodate those we love. We learn their presence like a new instrument, new language, or new favorite song. Our bodies and brains prepare a place for their presence inside of us in a very real and profound way. We are designed to become functioning parts of each other, and they become a habit that makes us the happiest we've ever been.

Withdrawal

The process of bonding and connecting to another person is extremely rewarding yet crippling. On one hand, you have been engulfed by excitement, joy, anticipation, and a level of closeness and familiarity you never dreamed possible. On the other hand, you have developed an almost codependent habit of them. When understanding how your body and brain cooperate to love them, losing them seems like it would destroy you.

When relationships are broken, you feel the loss on a cellular level. You are mentally, emotionally, and physically under attack by that loss. Your brain and your body will experience withdrawal symptoms as it desperately seeks the connection of the person you've become emotionally dependent on. Just like your body experiences a rush of chemicals as it begins to fall in love, the chemicals now cause your emotions to scramble around from the panic and the pain of loss. You will ride an emotional rollercoaster of sadness, anger, depression, denial, guilt, shame, embarrassment, and hurt. Physical pain may even present as your brain tries to translate that emotional hurt into something tangible that can be remedied. In other words, your body literally aches for them.

Brokenness is a natural response to the loss of a relationship, and your body is just as disturbed by this brokenness as you are. Even if you're decidedly done with them, regardless of what they've done or how badly they've treated you, your body is desperately trying to hold on to them. This is why you find yourself letting them go and then letting them back in again. It's a constant fight for and against that soul-tie. It's hard to let go, and brokenness is the natural result of not being able to let go.

Symptoms of heartache and brokenness can include but are not limited to:

- Anxiety
- Restlessness
- Irritability
- Insomnia
- Headaches
- Poor concentration
- Depression
- Deep sadness
- Social isolation
- Physical or phantom pains
- Stress cardiomyopathy (i.e. the physical heart is in pain and shows some of the same symptoms of a heart attack,

 a.k.a. the broken heart syndrome).

The list isn't exhaustive, but this gives you an idea of the effect that a broken heart can have on you. Now that you know some of the repercussions of broken soul-ties, the following exercise will help you to see how you've been broken. It will give you a clear picture of the changes you've gone through due to heartbreak. Complete the *Brokenness Assessment* on the next page to help you assess and give you a full picture of the heartache you are or have been experiencing.

"

Experiencing intimate relationships is far more than just wanting someone to hang with or sleep next to. It's a physical, emotional, biochemical, neurological, habitual bond.

BROKENNESS ASSESSMENT

Rate each symptom of brokenness that you either have previously experienced or are currently experiencing. Use 1 to indicate rarely or never and 5 to indicate frequently.

(circle one)

Anxiety	1	2	3	4	5
Restlessness	1	2	3	4	5
Irritability	1	2	3	4	5
Insomnia	1	2	3	4	5
Little or no appetite	1	2	3	4	5
Headaches	1	2	3	4	5
Poor concentration	1	2	3	4	5
Emotional numbness	1	2	3	4	5
Random bouts of sadness	1	2	3	4	5
Physical pain	1	2	3	4	5
Chest pain	1	2	3	4	5
Social isolation	1	2	3	4	5
Staying busy to avoid thinking	1	2	3	4	5
Self-medicate with food, drugs, or alcohol	1	2	3	4	5

*Completing this exercise is not a clinical diagnosis. It is a way for you to examine yourself and identify any potential concerns. It's important that you pay close attention to any strong or prolonged brokenness symptoms. They're telling you to seek the help of a physician or professional counselor.

RECAP: What Are True Soul-Ties?

Soul-ties are God's design for how we become one. It is how we emotionally, mentally, and physically bond in an intimate relationship. Those who we bond with become so much a part of our lives and our body, that they become a habit. And when the soul-tie is broken, we are hurt deeply.

"Above all else, guard your heart, for everything you do flows from it."
Proverbs 4:23 (NIV)

When the heart is infected with brokenness, your reality is affected. It may take a physical toll on your body while your actions and thoughts become overwhelmed by sadness, anger, despondency, or even apathy. What initially changed you for the better is now breaking you, and all you want to do is feel better. Your body will sometimes stop at nothing to make you feel better. You'll want to call them. You'll want to reach out and feel them next to you. You'll want to understand why and seek closure from them. You'll wish for them to reach out and apologize for everything that they've done to you so that you can receive them again. That will be your heart switch responding. This next assignment will help remind you to switch on your brain instead.

PHASE ONE EXERCISES

Phase one lays a lot of information on you fast and heavy. So take a moment and take a deep breath. Reflect on everything you just learned. Take a deep breath in, and then breathe it all out.

The next phase is going to go deeper into everything that you are experiencing, and it will likely get heavier for you emotionally. So right now, we are going to build your Soul-Ties Detox First Aid Kit.

Your first aid kit will have simple tools to help you when times get tough. When you're sad, when you feel like throwing this book in the trash (it happens), or when you miss them . . . use any of these tools, in case of emergency.

Your Soul-Ties Detox First Aid Kit

1. **Your Detox Playlist**—For when you need a "pick-me-up."
   - Open up Spotify, Apple Music, or even YouTube, and create a playlist. Be sure to name it something that represents you.
   - Then add all the songs that get you hyped and excited.
   - Whenever you feel yourself slipping into a place of sadness, shame, or regret, break out your playlist. Let it accompany you on a walk if you'd like.
2. **Write a love letter to yourself: For when you miss them.**
   - This will help when you need to turn your "heart switch" off.
   - We've added a template below.
   - Write it out, but take a picture of it and keep it on your phone so you always have it handy.
   - Read it every time you want to quit this journey go back to toxic relationships.

3. **Ten affirmations: For when you get discouraged.**
    - Recite these out loud to yourself whenever your journey gets difficult.
    - Take a picture of the affirmations and keep them on your phone.
    - Use them as often as you need to.

A LOVE LETTER TO MYSELF

For When I Miss Them or Believe They Will Change

Dear _____
      (insert your name)

I know you love them. And at times, it truly feels like they love you too. But it's time you're honest with yourself.

_____ makes you feel
(write their name)

> Write down how their actions and treatment have made you feel?

Every time they convince you that they will go back to being who you fell in love with, they . . .

> Remind yourself of the disappointments. What did they do that let you know that they weren't going to change?

They don't deserve you because

> Speak life into yourself right here...

Even when you don't feel like it, you are going to finish this process and fight for your peace. Because, if you don't do something right now . . .

> What will or won't happen if you don't keep going?

I love you. I'm here for you. And I will show up every day for you.

Love Always

_____

Sign and Date

10-AFFIRMATIONS FOR WHEN I GET DISCOURAGED

My healing journey is mine, and it doesn't have to look like anyone else's.

For the sake of my peace and my sanity, I cannot afford to lose control. But on the days that I do, I will dust myself off and begin again.

My peace is non-negotiable. They can't have it.

Love doesn't stop flowing just because I'm moving on. It's okay if I still love them, I just can't let my love for them lead me anymore.

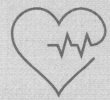

I am not abandoning them by choosing me. I am abandoning the fears that make me choose them over me.

10-AFFIRMATIONS FOR WHEN
I GET DISCOURAGED

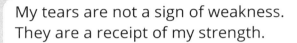

My tears are not a sign of weakness.
They are a receipt of my strength.

I will no longer participate in conversations
where my voice doesn't matter.

I will believe their patterns over
their promises.

My new boundaries are for me as much as
they are for them. I must stay safe.

I am forgiven. I am fearless. I am loved.
I will say this until I believe it.

You are still in week one. Please continue on to Phase Two.

Notes

Notes

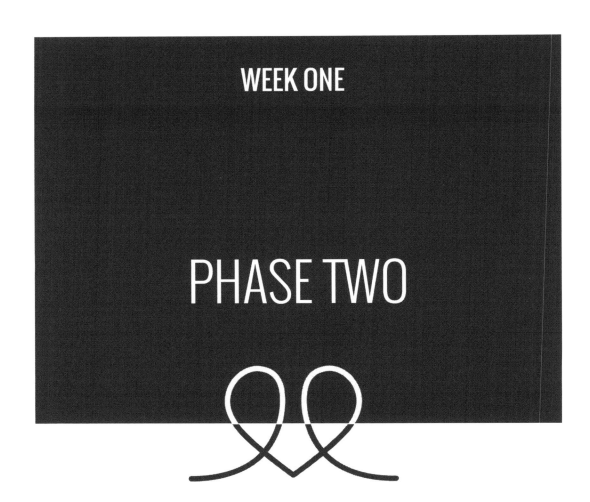

WEEK ONE

PHASE TWO

THE TIES THAT
BREAK US

"The Lord heals the brokenhearted and binds up their wounds."
Psalm 146:3 (NIV)

Phase Two: The Ties That Break Us

Phase one showed us just how powerful intimate relationships can be and how God designed us for relationships as a physical reflection of his spiritual oneness. We saw how those relationships changed us as bonds were made, and how destructive breaking those bonds can be. This is what we refer to as soul-ties.

While soul-ties are not technically addictions, your body sometimes responds to the breaking of these bonds much like it does to addictions. You may obsess over them as a way to cope with loss and heartbreak. You may go through emotional and physical ups and downs like withdrawal. Your body, mind, and heart do not want to accept that this is the end of the relationship. This is precisely when the bond becomes a bondage. You're not just struggling against how you were treated; you're also struggling against yourself. Quite frankly, it's torture.

The Ties That Break Us

Trust is a good thing. It is an innate part of how we are built. Most of us have the ability to meet a person and trust them without them even having to earn it. That's what makes betrayal so devastating. Betrayal takes advantage of the trust you gave so willingly and crushes it. The ironic thing about betrayal is that it cannot exist without trust. Some of the greatest pain we will ever experience will be because we opened ourselves up to trust and intimacy.

Soul-ties aren't bad because they're intimate, trusting, and open to oneness. They only become "bad" because they are broken and hurt us so badly. We call the heartache of betrayed soul-ties "broken ties." Broken ties are the broken bonds of an intimate relationship. These bonds are some of the hardest to let go of, either because of what that person has meant to us or because of what their rejection has done to us. When broken ties happen, we are seeking to salvage ourselves, our value, and our esteem as well as avoid the pain and humiliation of the loss. There are different types of relationships that can expose us to the pain of broken ties. We've isolated these relationships into the three general categories we see affecting people the most.

The Brokenhearted Ties

These are from soul-ties developed during a romantic intimate relationship. It doesn't matter if you were married or not. You've bonded in an intimate way due to the time that you spent with them and the process of connecting to them. They have become a part of you and you have devoted mental, emotional, and physical effort to maintaining this intimate relationship with them.

The investments that you've made into them and into the idea of them are substantial. Even after they've hurt you or after a break-up, you cannot seem to completely let go of everything that you've given to that relationship. Letting go of it all makes you feel as if you've been robbed. You paid a great cost for this dream, and now they are taking it away from you. Dreams, hopes, and "what ifs" turn into "whys," hurt, bitterness, and resentment. Yet and still, no matter how angry you are, you can't let go of them.

Broken hearts leave residual influence. Not only are you going through the mental trauma of losing someone, but you are also still vulnerable to manipulation by that same person. Residual connections mean that they still have a room for rent in your head and your heart. They still hold some form of influence over your thoughts and your behavior. Even when you genuinely try to move on, you feel trapped because moving on means accepting loss and defeat. And it hurts.

The Broken-Spirited Ties

The soul-tie here has to do with the unique relationship that you have with yourself. God's desire is that you see yourself with splendor, wonder, and worth, that you acknowledge your intrinsic value, and that you know what you deserve and don't deserve.

"I praise you because I am fearfully and wonderfully made; your works are wonderful, I know that full well." **Psalm 139:14 (NIV)**

When you no longer see your worth, when you stop believing what God says about you, you may be suffering from what we call a broken-spirited tie. It's almost like breaking up with yourself. You give up your right to everything good and amazing because you don't believe you deserve it. You've stopped believing in your value to such a degree that you no longer see why anyone else would value you. When the spirit is broken, self-loathing, self-pity, self-hate, and self-destruction show up.

There are many reasons why someone would get to this place of self-abandonment. The little boy or little girl who grew up in a toxic household. The person who wound up in a series of relationships that always left them feeling unlovable. The rape or sexual abuse survivor who never quite got over the shame. The person who left an abusive relationship so inwardly abused that they've started to believe the lies of their abuser. Whether it is a result of something done to them or something they've done, those suffering from these types of ties tend to seek love and validation from everywhere outside of themselves.

It's important to understand that a broken-spirited tie is beyond being disappointed in yourself. It's beyond being humbled by a life event. It's even beyond being humiliated. It's succumbing and surrendering to the lowest perception of yourself. A broken-spirited tie will have you oppressed by guilt and shame to such a degree you feel unfit for love. Yet you will still search for it in some way.

The reason why we consider this a soul-tie is because it has to do with your connection to yourself. No matter how you got here, allowing yourself to stay here is running the risk of perpetuating a cycle where you will punish yourself (and allow others to punish you) every time you start to believe you deserve more.

No matter what broken-tie a person has, it is quite common

for many to arrive at low points that mimic what we've described in the area of broken-spirited ties. But if you find yourself exclusively and deeply in this category of brokenness, don't stop at this book. The best help for you will definitely be counseling. You'll need a counselor who can help guide you hand in hand from that place of self-degradation back to a healthy you. You've already made the first step by grabbing this book. Keep going; there's hope for you.

If you find yourself at that dark place where you see no answers or no way out, and you've contemplated the idea of suicide, give yourself an opportunity to recover. Please call: 1-800-273-8255.

The Broken-Family Ties

For many of us, the earliest bonds we form are those within our families and with loved ones. With family being in our lives during our most formative years, we are the most vulnerable with them because everything about the environments they set shapes us. Being denied love, being rejected, being constantly criticized, or being emotionally or physically abused all have the potential of causing us to form broken-family ties. It's being subject to neglect and abandonment by those who we had no choice in trusting to keep us safe, and they abdicated their responsibility to do so.

Broken-family ties are particularly dangerous because they establish our standard of what we learn to accept and receive as love. Many times, people will find themselves in toxic or abusive relationships and will beat themselves up because they keep accepting poor treatment. Not realizing that much of what they have come to understand or receive as love can be traced back to those who shaped them. It is the effects of broken-family ties that seem to make it acceptable to be mistreated by a significant other, or to mistreat them.

Broken-family ties consist of all the people we have close, non-romantic relationships with. This includes family members, friends, teachers, mentors, coaches, and even spiritual leaders. Since this era of connections includes our formative years, it will include other children that molded us socially. This can include playmates and childhood bullies.

Broken-family ties have a particularly strong grip over us because we are held captive by a misguided sense of loyalty. Due to this loyalty, we begin the habit of chasing acceptance while simultaneously enduring pain because we believe we are supposed to. We then suffer a cognitive dissonance, trying to make what we are experiencing acceptable or excusable, even though we know that it is not. This is how we learn to invent the "good" in people who are really not good to us.

Broken-family ties can be the most destructive because they are usually the genesis of other issues. Due to the family connection, a person may either intensely protect a family member that has made their pain possible or they will intensely hate that family member due to the pain. Then they carry that pain, behavior, and acceptance of that behavior into other intimate relationships, often resulting in destructive, toxic relationship cycles.

Whichever form of pain or behavior exists, it is usually accompanied by a continuing need to seek the neglected love and acceptance that they never received from their family. Broken-family ties establish toxic cycles of love and loyalty in our adult lives.

There are a variety of experiences that fall into these three categories of broken soul-ties. Begin thinking about the primary category of your broken soul-tie. Is it an ex-lover that broke your heart? Perhaps it's someone close to you that you trusted that broke a bond. Maybe you've been through so much that you've not only begun questioning yourself, but you now actually dislike yourself. Or could it be a combination? Take a moment and find where you were broken and who did it. Then name the dominant broken soul-tie.

About Love

Whether you were in love with someone or you still love them, we are not here to make you fall out of love or stop loving whoever hurt you. No one can do that. Our goal is to show you how to acknowledge that love while not allowing love to be an excuse to keep you bound. We want you to be able to put your love for them in its proper place and then move forward, despite it.

The love you have for them is genuine. Inside of that authentic love for them, there exists your habit of their presence. The process of breaking this habit will seem to hurt more than the pain of staying in the relationship or tolerating them. You will be uncomfortable. You will get lonely. You will get tired of monitoring your behavior. You most definitely will feel weak at times. But don't give up.

Answer this simple question: Do you still love them?

Be honest with yourself. It's okay if the answer is yes. We want you to face and accept your feelings. Ignoring them will only hinder your progress.

Grieving Love

If you're truly honest with yourself, the real reason you're here is to make the pain go away. That's what people typically want when they seek help. You want the pain to subside as quickly and as easily as possible. You don't want to love them. You don't want to want them around. You don't want to cry anymore. You don't want the person who hurt you to have had the power to make you cry. This is grief.

It may seem like an odd thing to say, but denying your sadness is still a way of maintaining a connection to them. That's because you're mentally and emotionally still fighting against wanting them. Relationships are funny like that. You don't have to like a person to be in a relationship with them. Every thought, every conversation you replay in your head, or every time you try to suppress your love for them by conjuring up hate for them is an interaction with them. The longer you're fighting against their presence in your head, the longer they will stay there.

Grieving the loss of them and the relationship empowers you. Lamentation (expressing grief or sorrow) helps the healing process and expedites the process of relieving your pain. Crying is power.

Intentionally taking time to grieve the loss of a relationship will do four things for you:

1. **Help you face the loss** – By facing the loss, you emotionally acknowledge that it is time to move forward. What once was, is no more.
2. **Help you accept the loss** – Accepting the loss is addressing the reality of the present. It moves you from a place of denial to a place of action.
3. **Help you bury the loss** – Burying the loss is your last act of laying the relationship to rest and walking away. It is the final resting place of everything you dreamed of and hoped for. If you've ever had to bury someone close to you, you know that the lowering of the coffin and watching the dirt begin to fill the hole in the ground where they are being laid to rest makes everything final. The burial forces you to move.
4. **Help you to purge the loss** – Purging is the process of being cleansed thoroughly. Crying it out isn't just an emotional outburst. Biochemically speaking, your tears serve the purpose of purging your stress. They release cortisol (the stress hormone) and aid in your release and your relief.

We use the metaphor of death because, quite frankly, that's how it feels. This is how your body is responding to it. Earlier in the book, we talked about how your neural networks rearrange themselves to accommodate a person in your brain. So when you don't use them, or when that person is no longer around to facilitate the connectivity of those neural networks, they actually die. The brain prunes itself of unused connections. In a very real way, you're burying something that is no longer a part of you. It becomes its own special type of hell because you can still pick up the phone and call that person.

We're going to give you a hard piece of truth here, but it must be said. Many people avoid the grieving process because a) they actually want to still feel connected to them in some way, or b) they know that if they truly take the time to grieve, it also means they are closing the door on the possibility of the relationship working out. The truth? Even if you rekindle the relationship, you nor them can be the same person that allowed or facilitated this hurt to begin with. So grieving is still necessary. The process of grief changes you. At least that's the hope.

Throughout this entire process, you will be grieving. You will do exercises that cause you to remember things you didn't want to remember. You'll be challenged to do things that will go against your normal mode of functioning. You'll be saddened, weakened, and sometimes feel sick. You will grieve during this journey, and that's okay. You're supposed to!

We want you to come out of this process a new you. But first, something has to die. Grieving the death of this relationship will help you live again. So, take your time—as much as you need—and grieve.

About Divorce

Divorce and the effects of divorce can be especially devastating. Marriages are supposed to be the most intimate safe havens. When the inner sanctuary of marriage is infiltrated, there is a feeling of being violated that lingers like smoke damage from a fire. A divorcee has to contend with feelings of abandoning or being abandoned by their significant other, and they also might feel abandoned by God. Why didn't God fix this? Why didn't He make them treat me right? Why didn't He save my marriage?

When going through divorce, you'll likely battle between anger, frustration, depression, and, at times, overwhelming accountability. Regardless of who did what in your marriage, seeing it end will make you feel like a failure. You may fluctuate between feeling unworthy because you couldn't keep your spouse and feeling like a fool because you believed God was a part of your marriage. Questions like "What's wrong with me?" "What did I do wrong?" or "How did I fail?" will dominate your thoughts. It will feel like being stuck between abandonment by God and being a disappointment to God, all at the same time.

We understand the confusion and the condemnation you may feel. Both of us were raised in Christian homes and have been taught how God hates divorce. Nevertheless, we have still both been divorced. It's not something we're proud of, but it's something we've made peace with. Here's how.

We've survived our own self-condemnation by understanding something crucial about divorce. Divorce, in the proper context, is deliverance. Understanding this has allowed us to help others who were suffering from the fallout of their own divorces. So, if you're one who feels guilt, shame, and failure, there's something we have to show you.

What You Need to Know About Divorce ———

1. **Divorce is not a sin** – Nowhere in the Bible does it say that divorce is a sin. NOWHERE! We know that God says that He hates divorce in Malachi 2:16. However, in studying that in context, we realized that God hates the cruelty a husband places upon his wife as a result of divorce, especially in the ancient setting in which this was said. Cruelty is what God hates, which is why he allowed for the bill of divorce.

Go back and reread it:

"For the Lord, the God of Israel, saith that he hateth putting away:[Divorce] for one covereth violence with his garment, saith the Lord of hosts: therefore take heed to your spirit, that ye deal not treacherously." Malachi 2:16 (KJV)

God hates "putting away" (divorce) because it ". . . covereth violence with his garment" (cruelty). The word garment is a metaphor for wife. The wife is the closest thing to his flesh, yet he's supposed to take care of her like a garment. In other words, abandoning the wife was cruel, violent, and abusive. Let's look at a different translation, namely the NIV:

"'The man who hates and divorces his wife,' says the Lord, the God of Israel, 'does violence to the one he should protect,' says the Lord Almighty. So be on your guard, and do not be unfaithful."

Divorce isn't the issue. Cruelty is the issue. Divorce is the means by which cruelty happened.

2. God would never suggest a sin as a remedy or punishment – God does not sin. If divorce was a sin, God would not have instructed Moses to develop the bill of divorce.

It's true, the bill of divorce that Moses was allowed to write was not in God's plan for marriage and oneness. However, it was a necessary provision to protect women from the cruelty of being arbitrarily abandoned by their husbands. In a patriarchal and chauvinistic society, only men could declare divorce. During that time, they were able to do so for trivial reasons. However, to declare divorce meant economic and social doom for the woman. When a man declared divorce, he was announcing her brokenness and inability to be a suitable wife, and he left her destitute and homeless. This is what was meant by cruelty.

What the bill of divorce did was salvage the woman's economic viability. She was able to leave with whatever land or wealth that came with her from her family. At minimum, a divorced and disgraced woman could survive economically in such a society. The bill of divorce prevented economic cruelty.

The bill of divorce may have also prevented the men from trafficking their wives. A husband would divorce his wife arbitrarily, and then give her to a friend to marry for a time. After that time, she would be divorced again and the former husband would remarry her. In a male-dominated society, this would be a way to circumvent the adultery law and traffick their wives. The bill of divorce protected women, making it illegal to remarry once divorced.

During ancient and barbaric times, God always sought to protect women from their social plights, and the bill of divorce is one such way. The bill of divorce was a protective covering to keep men from taking advantage of women. It was an attempt to curtail the misuse of divorce in marriage.

Now, with that said, let's be honest, not everyone gets a divorce for the right reasons. Both marriage and divorce are still being misused. Just understand that the sin is found in the intention, not in divorce itself. At worst, divorce is used to sin; at best, divorce is a plan of deliverance.

Divorce is Not a Sin ────────────────────

Your spouse's behavior was not your fault. Their choices were theirs. Abandonment, neglect, abuse, mistreatment, mismanagement of emotion or financial resources, or infidelity were things done to you. You did not do those things to yourself. Yes, it's important to own your part of the breakdown of a relationship, but it's important that you never mistake their behavior as something to take ownership for. You are not at fault for what they chose to do to destroy the relationship. You walking away so that you could mentally, emotionally, and physically survive is the consequence of their behavior.

Your divorce was deliverance from cruelty. God loved you in it and still loves you today. He could not make you make a decision that you didn't want to make, nor could He control your spouse. But what God could do is continue to leave a way for you to survive the ordeal. God does love you and it's not despite your divorce. He loves you through your divorce.

God understands your pains. He knows how you got there and who did it. He loves you in that pain, just like he loved you through that circumstance. He knows the mistakes that you've made, and He loves you despite them. God wants your safety, survival, peace, and freedom.

Remember this: God loves you. God delivered you. He is still delivering you. That's why you're here.

The Uncomfortable Issue of Sin ────────────

We did not want to write a book about healing and only use God as a peripheral figure. While we are attending to the matters of your heart, it's important that we present the desires of God's heart to you as well. Yes, He desires for you to be healed, whole, and delivered. But more important to God than deliverance from this current situation is your ultimate deliverance above all.

Your life today is a culmination of happenstance, thoughts, and actions over time. And while this program is about addressing some of the things that have been done to you, we wanted to take this small portion to address the areas within you that may have been spiritually out of order. If you find that you have misused and abused God's beautiful creation that is you; if you recognize patterns of behavior that have widened the distance between you and God; if you have engaged in activity that has broken your covenant with God; then a big part of your healing journey must include getting back into alignment with God.

Salvation begins with us admitting that we are sinners, yet believing in a loving God that won't make us suffer the consequences of sin. God loved us enough to provide a payment for us. That's why Christ is the Savior. He redeems us from the consequences of sin and presents us to God so that we may dwell in relationship with Him. Read Romans 10:8-11.

This is how Christ becomes our Lord and Savior. Being born again doesn't mean that we won't make mistakes. It means that we are alive, with an opportunity to grow in Christ. As such, we must be willing to recognize mistakes when we make them. We confess them, change our minds about them, and turn away from them.

Before you get started with this next week, if you are not a believer in Christ, we would like you to become a believer and receive salvation. If you are a believer but have fallen away, come back home and embrace your Father once again. We also encourage you to find a good community of believers willing to help you grow in the way of Christ.

If you desire to dedicate or rededicate your life to Christ, read the following prayer:

God, I know that I am a sinner.
My thoughts, actions, and feelings have been far from you.
I have done things that I am not proud of.
I am not clean.
But I don't want to die.
I cannot pay this price.
God, I do want to live.
I want to live as your child belonging to you.
I receive your gift for me.
I receive the sacrifice of Christ's life for my life.
I receive Christ's death for my sins, as my payment.
Cleanse me now of my guilt before you, God.

Now I receive the resurrection of Christ as my own.
I live guilt free because Christ lives.
As Christ died for me, I live for Christ.
I would like Christ's mind, heart, and goals in me.
Please send the Helper—the Holy Spirit—to me, Father, so that I can live this renewed life to your glory!

Congratulations! Even in the privacy of your home, the heavens celebrate your life!

Final Words For This Week: ————————————

You Will Not Leave Empty Handed

The book of Exodus is not just about escaping the oppressor in Pharaoh. It's also about how God facilitated and funded the escape of Israel through their oppressor. When God called Moses to aid in Israel's deliverance, God told him that not only will Israel be delivered, but that they would not leave empty handed. Yes, the people of Egypt paid Israel as they left.

Your oppressor wants to be your god and will attempt to keep you captive. For some, your oppressor will be angry that they can no longer control you. Some oppressors will try their best to turn other people against you. Don't give up. Keep going forward and don't look back.

This journey will be your exodus, your escape from those who hurt you. It's going to get uncomfortable for a bit, but at least you won't be where you were. And guess what? You will not leave empty handed. Whoever tried to hurt you has provided you with a wealth that cannot be denied: your testimony.

During the Soul-Ties Detox, you will face some obstacles and go through great grieving. We want you to keep a journal to help you get through each of the weekly phases. The first week is prerequisite education. The second week is the physical battle. The third and fourth week is the mental and emotional battle. The fifth week is the emotional and spiritual battle. The sixth week is the week of burial.

At the end of the detox, your journal will have chronicled each week resulting in your story. Your testimony will be the story of your journey from oppression to freedom. It will chronicle your actions, struggles, and progress. It will remind you where you came from while encouraging others that they can make it too.

You may not feel like it now, but your story will give so many people hope. Hundreds, maybe thousands, will be touched by the wealth of your testimony. In the end, their attempt at destroying you will have made you stronger.

It is our great honor and privilege to be a part of that testimony. It is our hope to help facilitate the telling of your story when you're done. We thank you. See you next week.

"

The Process Of
Breaking This
Habit Will Seem
To Hurt More Than The
Pain Of Staying In The
Relationship Or Tolerating
Them.

SmallGroupDiscussionQuestions

1. What have you learned about how soul-ties affect you?
2. What type of tie do you feel has broken you?
3. What (if any) was the hardest brokenness symptom that you've experienced?
4. What type of accountability will you need from this group in order to help you finish this program successfully?

This is the end of week one. We've included a journal prompt before you begin week two. When you have some downtime alone, take a moment to write. Then take time to rest. Don't forget to finish your first aid kit, in case of emergency.

Journal Prompt

───────── ✏ ─────────

Before you begin journaling, we want you to imagine going to sleep tonight and a miracle happening while you are sleeping. When you wake in the morning, you are healed, your hurt has completely gone away, and your life is in an altogether happier place. It's as if you were never broken. Go ahead. Close your eyes for a second and imagine that as you breathe in and out. Now, write about that day. What do you do when you wake up? What car do you drive to work? Where are you working? What's your position at work? How does being in control of your life make you feel? How do you know you're healed? Don't just talk about what you feel on this day, but about what you do. What are you doing differently in this totally healed and peaceful state? Write about it.

Journal Exercise

Write about the morning you wake-up completely healed.

Journal Exercise Cont.

Journal Exercise Cont.

PHASE THREE

THE FLUSH AND
THE FAST

———— ༄ ————

"Is not this the kind of fasting I have chosen: to loose the chains of injustice and untie the cords of the yoke, to set the oppressed free and break every yoke?" **Isaiah 58:6 (NIV)**

Phase Three: Flush and Fast

Breaking the Habit of Them

The fact that someone has become your habit doesn't mean that you're out of control. It means that they have become so much a part of you that, as long as there is an attachment to them, your brain will randomly search for them. When someone is a habit to you, your brain will inadvertently engage with them in thought or emotion as an involuntary response to missing them. As uncomfortable as they are or the relationship with them was, they have become your comfort zone. So to counteract your natural reaction to missing them, you need a new comfort zone. It's time to create a new norm.

Athletes, and those who are physically active, usually work out with a goal in mind. Whether it's to gain weight or lose it, they create a routine to facilitate achieving that goal. But every so often, some have complained of reaching a plateau where they suddenly stop losing or gaining weight. Their body has grown so accustomed to their routine that it is no longer a challenge. They will need to "shock the system" by completely changing their workout regimen. It puts the body back in a position to learn something new that will accomplish their goal.

What you're about to embark on will shock your system. It

will be incredibly uncomfortable at first, because it requires something new. Like any habit that needs changing, the first action is to remove yourself from whatever perpetuates the habit. The reality of the matter is that you (your brain) are wired for what you're used to. Simple thoughts can evoke hormones, neural transmitters, cognitive functions, and feelings. Everything that has helped you bond or attach to them is now effectively a part of you. We can't remove you from yourself. We can't hypnotize you so you act like someone else. Instead, we're going to help you purge your environment in a way that helps facilitate change in you. Are you ready to shock your system?

Removing the Catalysts Around You

When I was trying to heal and break free from soul-ties, I felt like I was failing at it every day. I was in a minute-by-minute drama where, at any moment, I could go from being perfectly fine and focused on me to having a complete meltdown. It didn't matter if I was at work or in the car taking my daughters to school, a meltdown was always just a thought, a song, or a conversation away. Everywhere I turned there was something that reminded me of him. I began to get so frustrated with myself that I actually began to express some of the most hurtful negative self-talk to myself.

You should have heard the things that I was saying to myself. "Uggh! Suck it up, Taccara. You are such a mess! What is wrong with you? You're all over the place like some dumb broad. Get it together!" And then I'd cry some more, only to repeat the cycle again the next time a thought, song, or conversation triggered me. What was it that kept me going in and out of emotional and mental breakdowns? I was unable to truly be free of the habit of my ex and his influence over my feelings because I was trying to carry on in my life normally as if nothing had changed, as if I had not just suffered a traumatic loss. Everything had changed. So I had to make some life adjustments to accommodate the change that was happening within me.

This part of the process will be all about creating a sterile environment for healing. Flushing and fasting will be the first steps of breaking the bond that you've built. There's a difference in the flushing and the fasting, so please follow along.

The *flushing* is where you permanently purge yourself and your living environment of the things and people that trigger you to respond to your habit (they who hurt you). Anything that triggers memories, emotions, or actions must be removed. You won't be able to control everything that triggers you. Some triggers really are intangible—being mental or emotional—and may provoke you without warning. Those will get better by maintaining a clean environment and flushing the tangible items in your life that negatively affect your ability to move on. What we want you to do is remove anything physical or tangible that provokes triggers.

Fasting is a necessary but temporary function. The fasting will require you to cut, reduce, or completely eliminate everything that hinders your healing process as well, just temporarily.

Just like a wound that can be contaminated by an unhealthy environment, you must isolate yourself from some things. This will challenge you to stay away from people, places, and things that have become a part of your norm but are reinforcing the habit(s) keeping you bound.

Fasting may also include people, places, or atmospheres that aren't a direct threat to you, but can be used indirectly to trigger your habit (i.e. gossiping friends, shared friends, shared worship facilities, places that hold memories, etc.). These are the people and things that may slow, pause, or halt your progress. Since they are obstacles, you will want to take a break from them during this journey as well.

Step 1: Break All Forms of Communication

"Do not be misled: 'Bad company corrupts good character.'"
1 Corinthians 15:33 NIV

We want you to consider everyone who has the potential to trigger you in your current emotional state. This doesn't just include those you are directly trying to detox from. This also includes those peripheral people in your life. They may not necessarily be bad for you. But they are not exactly healthy for you either.

No calls; no text messages; no social media stalking; no commenting on social media posts; no subliminal posts or memes about them; no DMs.

- Block them.
- Delete their number.
- Unfriend and unfollow them.

Cut them off completely.

When it comes to breaking free, many don't like this part of the process because it requires you to break pieces of you as well. If you've ever broken your arm or your leg, you might recall the need for doctors to reset the broken bone. In order for the bone to heal properly, doctors have to manipulate the broken ends of the bone and place them back into their original position. This can sometimes be even more painful than the break itself. When cutting people off completely, it feels like you are breaking your heart all over again. You're essentially denying yourself all the things that keep you connected—the things that give you a bit of hope—but it must be done so you can heal.

What If My Ex and I Have Children Together?

If you have children together, there are several reasons why the idea of cutting your ex off might give you anxiety.

1. This will be your first time creating or setting up boundaries, and you're afraid of making them feel rejected or coming off as the "bad guy" in this new norm.
2. You've tried this before but they became forceful and

almost belligerent when you tried to enforce boundaries.

3. You know that once you do set up and enforce boundaries, it sort of closes the door on the possibility of rekindling the relationship.

4. When you set up boundaries, they punish you by becoming parental liabilities. Either they stop being dependable or they are not allowing the parent-child relationship to flourish.

Regardless of what may give you pause in this step, it's important that you keep in mind why you're doing it. You are in a very real hell, and their persistent, unregulated access to you hinders your growth. Using your child as an opportunity to punish you or as leverage against you simply proves how dirty they really are. Remember, you are not responsible for their behavior.

Here are several ways to handle communication and visitation when children are involved.

Direct Child-to-Parent Communication – If you have children that are old enough to have their own mobile devices, allow the child to speak directly to their parent about what's going on in their lives, updates on activities, etc. At this age (12+), your child should be able to understand that the subject of the conversation should be about them and nothing that is going on outside of them.

Conversations about your personal life, work, and outside activities are off-limits. This works both ways;

conversations about your ex's personal life through the child are also off-limits. Your child or children are not go-betweens or spies. The ex has no right to ask the child about you, and you have no right to question your child(ren) about them. As long as the children are safe, as long as they are happy, allow the relationship with their other parent to be guided by their new norm.

If you find that your ex is not adhering to these rules and they are emotionally manipulating your children to try to gain sympathy from them by sharing details about your break-up, consult a therapist that will be willing to intervene and testify before the courts, if necessary. This type of manipulation can be considered abusive at worse, or emotionally devastating in the least.

Limit Unnecessary Contact – When you have younger children that do not have their own phones, there will most certainly be times when you'll have to speak to the other parent. If this is the case, it's important for you to establish boundaries for every conversation.

Commit to only communicating about the child or children, and make no exceptions. You may be cordial and exchange pleasantries, but keep the conversation moving forward within those boundaries. *We'll provide an exercise later to help you create concrete boundaries for yourself.*

If you find that the other parent continues to push boundaries and refuses to respect them, there's an app for that. There are several co-parenting apps that facilitate the exchange of important information regarding the children without you having to come in direct contact with each other all the time (if at all).

These apps are:
- OurFamilyWizard
- Cozi
- WeParent
- Coparently
- Custody Connection
- Parentship
- 2Houses

The use of apps like these remove another layer of control from your ex. It's likely that they have never experienced you standing up for yourself or taking control of your situation in this way, so they will not initially take you seriously. That's okay. You are having to retrain them just as you are retraining yourself in this process. Implementing this extra layer of boundaries will help you see just how far they will go in maintaining access to you or control over you. Their unwillingness to respect your boundaries will let you know if you need to take it to the next level.

Consider The Help of a Mediator – When it comes to visitation arrangements (if they are cordial enough to agree to something), the first thing we suggest is to attempt to calmly create a plan for visitation with the children. When it's time to pick up or drop off the children, consider using a mediator to facilitate transportation. This keeps your interaction with them to a minimum.

These can be willing parties who care for your children and desire to see them minimally impacted by the demise of your relationship. Consider mutual friends, parents, grandparents, or any willing family member that you trust and who will not engage in any conversation outside of the needs and welfare of the children. Whoever you designate should be fully supportive of this process.

Court-Appointed or Voluntary Mediation – If you are in a situation where your ex does not want to adhere to healthy boundaries or comply with any form of visitation agreements you try to set, you may want to consider involving a court-appointed mediator or find one on your own to facilitate a legal agreement. While this process will likely cost you both, it will help establish a more legally binding agreement that you can use in conjunction with your newly formed boundaries.

This will jolt them at first, and they might even feel betrayed that you are attempting to involve the law. It is fine to reiterate that their unwillingness to work with you is what led to this, but do not allow them to guilt you out of doing what is best for you and the children. This simply lets them know that you are serious about the boundaries that you want to establish, and it sends a clear message about where you are.

Passive aggression can also be an issue with your ex. When they begin to see that you are serious about your boundaries, passive aggression is their only weapon or recourse. Not being available for the kids when they agreed to or dodging attempts to connect with the kids are all common in situations like these.

If your ex begins to evade responsibility for the kids by becoming passive aggressive with you, don't set yourself up to depend on them. Don't try to force them to do what they know they are supposed to do. Make them your plan B until they prove they are anything else. Passive aggression reinforces the control they are losing, and by chasing them to be who they are supposed to be, you will fall right into their hand. Have other plans and people that you can count on outside of them. The quickest way to suck the oxygen out of their flame is to position yourself to not need them. This way, you're never totally caught off guard and feeling out of control if they behave this way. You've got this.

Word to the wise here. You will need your PSS or your small group during this time. When you are not used to standing up for yourself, it will be extremely hard. Being assertive will seem foreign to you. Your ex won't like this either. You will be made to feel like you are the villain for finally choosing you. Your boundaries and your patience may constantly be tested. Even after you've given your all, you may begin to feel guilty for walking away and not trying harder. nd there may be times where you will begin to feel like it may be easier to simply give in and let your ex have their way. Call your PSS and allow them to remind you that this is the only way you get your power back.

Yes. You're Going to Have to Break Up With the Kids, Too.

If you've dated someone that has bonded with your child, or you have bonded with theirs, you may have to let that go as well. It's an unfortunate truth, but the loss of the relationship with the child(ren) will sometimes have to be a casualty of the break-up, especially in dating. The reason is because children can be used as an unnecessary bridge to keep the relationship door open. What will happen is you (or your ex) will begin to inadvertently use the child as a tool or a weapon to maintain connection. Even if it's unintentional, it's easy for this to happen when emotions are involved.

Also, remember that your version of this break-up is not the children's version. They don't feel what you feel, because they didn't experience what you experienced. Don't project your emotions onto the children, thinking they share them. They don't. Children are resilient and are probably dealing with the break-up far better than you. They may not understand everything that is going on in the beginning, but they will get it in time.

During my divorce, my ex-husband (who never really cared to build a relationship with my kids) decided that he was going to start hanging out with my daughters, taking them bowling, and having "serious chats" with them about our impending divorce. While I won't try to understand the motives behind his new-found interest in my daughters (though I have ideas), what I refused to do was allow him to try to build a relationship with my daughters that would enable him to emotionally manipulate them or keep him connected to me in any way. It was hard, but as I was establishing my boundaries, I had to ask him to stop engaging with my children in ways that he hadn't done in the years that we were married.

There will be instances of divorce or long-term relationships where you've been a part of the children's lives for an extended period of time, and perhaps you've even helped raise them (or vice versa). We would advise you to treat this the same way you would if you shared the children biologically. While you won't necessarily have to set up formal visitation or custody agreements, perhaps you will want to still communicate with the children and schedule visits or play dates.

In these cases, we recommend that you begin by talking to the biological parent and asking them what their comfort level is with you communicating with their child. If you are the biological parent, it is up to you to identify your comfort level with that relationship continuing as well. Once you've established your comfort levels and set up some ground rules for the relationships, consider using the apps and tools mentioned above. The goal is to ensure even these relationships do not disrupt your healing journey.

Key questions to ask yourself before proceeding with this relationship with the child(ren):

1. What was the relationship with the children like before the break-up or divorce? Would continuing this relationship be foreign to them or seem odd to them?
2. If it's your child, will the child be negatively affected by their inability to see your ex? Are they crying and begging to see them or spend time with them?
3. Can you honestly say that the motives in wanting to maintain a relationship with the child(ren) are solely based on the child and not to keep a relationship going with you or the other parent?
4. Does your ex really want a relationship with them? *Make sure you aren't trying to force prolonged connection to them by using the children.*
5. Has your ex honored your boundaries up until now in a way that makes you feel comfortable with continuing the relationship with the child(ren)? Can you be sure they won't begin to use the child against you?

How Do I Cut Them Off if We Live Together?

Going through this process while living with them is not a good idea and can be ultimately dangerous for you, especially if the person is already toxic or abusive. You might be able to emotionally disconnect from them, but that's about it. Remember, this is a detox. You're not only rejecting them, but you're ejecting them from your life. Doing that with them there will most certainly come off as antagonizing and insulting.

Instead, we recommend that you dissolve the relationship and leave (or have them leave) before trying to effectively detox from them. This is the safest solution for you and anyone involved.

Be Prepared to Use the Law

It's always surprising for people to hear that the soul-tie works both ways. Just because they aren't crying, begging you to come back, or showing signs of emotional distress does not mean that they aren't suffering from this loss. It just looks different. Persistent confrontation, control, and influence over you is how that soul-tie presents. And they will stop at nothing to maintain that influence, or at least show you that they can control you whenever they want. Controlling you is part of their norm, and when you begin to set up boundaries, they process it like you are literally taking something from them.

Do not underestimate their dependency upon your presence, especially if they have been toxic or have ever been remotely abusive. As much as you think you know them, and as harmless as they have been up until now, you have never seen them losing you in such an absolute way. You will begin to see them go through changes and exhibit behavior that reflects their desperation. This is not just exes. This includes family that desires to control you as well.

Before I met Taccara, my ex and I were married for 12 years. I took my role as a husband and protector very seriously, even if my marriage wasn't perfect. One person who was not entirely thrilled about my position as a husband was my mother. For all my natural life she had unfiltered access to me and my children. She was able to come and go as she pleased. She was able to make decisions about my life and my children's lives. But when I became a husband, that all changed, and she was furious about it. I kept brushing her off, assuming that she would get it if I just ignored her, but she only grew more furious and continued to test my boundaries.

My sweet mother went from being my biggest advocate to one of my greatest enemies during that time. The biggest mistake that I made was that I underestimated the lengths she would go to regain the control she once had. My desire for freedom, even as a grown man, became a threat to her identity. My underestimation of my mother, and the subsequent events that followed, led to a ten-year period where I was estranged from my mother. Had I initiated boundaries earlier in the process, I would have had time to observe her ability to honor my boundaries and escalate my response to her if necessary.

You're likely going to see a side of that person you've never seen before. Whatever their prior behavior was, it is liable to escalate. They can become more verbally or physically abusive. They may use friends, family, or children as leverage to fight against you. They may even attempt to use fear to recapture you. You need to be willing to protect yourself and your family at all costs. Use the law.

Protective Orders – You must be serious about your sanity and your safety. Do not hesitate to get a protective order if they are being aggressively uncooperative. This includes harassment by texts, calls, social media, stalking, or showing up to your job or home. Any means that they can use to force their presence on you (especially after you requested they stop) should be considered a form of aggression against you. Most jurisdictions have anti-stalking laws; look into them.

Make sure your conversations are well documented and recorded. Keep records of you telling any aggressor to leave you alone. This will require you to either stop answering phones and restricting communication to text or downloading an app to record your phone conversations.

Keep all texts, emails, and DMs and potentially look into indoor and outdoor video recording and monitoring devices like Ring™, Wyze™, D-Link™, and Arlo™. Make sure that your experiences with the unrelenting person can be recorded and clearly shared in a court of law. We'd even advise you to keep copies on a cloud where you can give access to a trusted friend to see and download in case of emergency.

Relocate – If you can afford it, move to an undisclosed location, either far away or with someone that makes you feel protected. Remember, this is for your mental and physical well-being. Do not gamble with your life. It's easy to believe that you know them. Even if they've never shown signs of abusive behavior before, a person has a greater propensity to snap at the thought of losing you. Do what you must to be safe.

Additionally, moving can be cleansing for you. Leaving the vicinity creates needed distance from an old, familiar environment. It puts you in a place of newness and offers sort of a fresh start. If it's available to you, moving is as much of an opportunity as it is a protection.

This all may seem like a bit much to some, but to those who are potentially breaking free from toxic or even narcissistic people, it's very necessary. Once you realize that you can only control yourself, your environment, and your peace, you have to account for every possible variable that may come to disrupt your environment. The goal with this is to review all areas in your life that could serve as a stumbling block in your journey or become potentially dangerous to you.

A Final Note on Breaking Communication With People

Taking the step towards removing your presence from people (cutting them off) can be empowering, but we want you to make sure that you do not do this hastily or as a way to simply get them to "act right." The moment that you use cutting them off as a weaponized ultimatum or tool for vengeance is the moment that you are being manipulative towards them. You don't want to reward them by meeting their dysfunction with mutual dysfunction. Go quietly and go in peace, even if going is not exactly peaceful.

FAQ's

What if people at work are toxic to my detox journey?
This will be tricky, but you can do this. Think of it like being on a diet when there's a potluck at work. In this scenario, your coworkers expect you to participate in the potluck, but participating conflicts with your diet. A coworker who is toxic to your detox journey is the same.

A toxic coworker will bring you things that you can't "eat." Their disposition, their gossip, their nosey questions, their boasting . . . whatever it is, you cannot participate in it. You have to have the attitude of "Thanks, but no thanks." Be cordial yet secluded. You do not have to air your business, but it's okay to communicate that you have private matters that demand your attention and focus right now. Keep smiling.

What if people at church are unhealthy for my detox journey?
You would be surprised that you're not the only one with that issue. While places of worship are supposed to be safe places for us, they're also a place where we tend to be the most vulnerable and open. Unfortunately, that also leaves us vulnerable and open to a culture of gossip, shame, ostracism, narcissism, etc. Whether you've ended a relationship with someone that attends your church or you're simply not comfortable due to the people at your church, it's okay to admit that the church (the building) may not be the best place for you.

Everyone in church is recovering from something. Without proper guidance, the church can be an incubation chamber for an environment of hurt. If you've been hurt, shamed, exploited, or possibly forcefully influenced by people in your church, you may need to make some changes.

Lack of safety in a place you're supposed to be the safest can be destructive to you and your faith. Here are a few options you may have.

- **Change the service that you attend** – Many churches these days have more than one service. If this is an option, change to an earlier or later service time.
- **Change your seating** – If you cannot change the time in which you enjoy service, choose seating that separates you from those who are an enemy to your journey. Maintaining a distance doesn't mean that they are getting their way. It means that you are protecting yourself, thus getting your way.
- **Change churches** – For many people, this is a last resort. However, remember that your loyalty is to Christ, not people. You'll need to find a place that works for you. When you do, go slow. Make sure that this is a good place for a new spiritual home. Do not seek replacements for the previous attachment(s) you're trying to break.
- **Virtual church** – After spending a year in quarantine due to the 2020 pandemic, this method may be more comfortable than ever. You might be sick of it, but it could be an excellent outlet. If this is available, enjoy your church from your computer or mobile device.

Keep in contact with a trusted leader in the ministry to let them know where you are. If you are comfortable enough, share your journey with them. If not, simply tell them that you are recovering from a private personal issue and will be back as soon as possible.

Should I be dating during this process? With love and concern, we implore you to not be dating right now. You are in no way fit for a relationship, otherwise you wouldn't be here. As good as a new love interest sounds to you, you would be using that person to circumvent the pain of detox.

You must dedicate and commit yourself to this process and get some degree of healing. Allowing others to be involved with you during this time will complicate matters and confuse the both of you. Do not do that to them. Do not do that to yourself. Anyone who is for you will want you to heal before you get into a relationship with them. Anyone who is for you will not force you to abort your healing for the sake of them.

What you need and desire as a broken person looks completely different than what you need and desire as a healed person. A broken person is seeking comfort, validation, and wound care for their emotional traumas. A healed person will be seeking something entirely different because their needs will not be clouded by their pain. Everything they need will have first been found within themselves and within God.

Wait until you can present the healed version of you to someone. It will be worth it.

The Soul-Ties Impact Assessment

In this exercise, we want you to evaluate the impact that your toxic soul-ties have on not just your mental and emotional state, but also on your entire life.

Take a look at each area and answer honestly if the area has been minimally, moderately, or severely impacted by this relationship. Complete this exercise for anyone that you're desiring to break free from.

1. How is my mental and emotional health impacted by my relationship with

_____ (Insert their Name)

☐ Minimally   ☐ Moderately   ☐ Severely

2. How is my spiritual health and growth impacted by my relationship with this person?

☐ Minimally   ☐ Moderately   ☐ Severely

3. How is my physical health impacted by my relationship with them?

☐ Minimally   ☐ Moderately   ☐ Severely

4. How are my familial relationships and friendships impacted by my relationship with them?

☐ Minimally   ☐ Moderately   ☐ Severely

5. How has my Job/Career/Personal Goals for life been impacted by my relationship with them?

☐ Minimally   ☐ Moderately   ☐ Severely

6. How has my joy for life been impacted by my relationship with them?

☐ Minimally   ☐ Moderately   ☐ Severely

The Soul-Ties Impact
Exercise

Now that you've assessed the impact of their influence in your life, let's look at what will happen if you stay connected to them. You don't need to use your imagination here. Use what you have come to know and understand about these toxic relationships and soul-ties.

What will happen (or continue to happen) to my mental and emotional health if I stay in this relationship? Write it out.

What will happen (or continue to happen) to my spiritual health and growth if I remain in this relationship? Write it out.

The Soul-Ties Impact
Exercise

What will happen (or continue to happen) to my physical health if I stay in this relationship? Write it out.

What will happen (or continue to happen) to familial relationships and friendships if I stay in this relationship? Write it out.

The Soul-Ties Impact
Exercise

What will happen (or continue to happen) to my job, career, or personal goals if I stay in this relationship? Write it out.

What will happen (or continue to happen) to my joy and love for life if I stay in this relationship? Write it out.

The Purpose for Assessing Soul-Ties Impact ——

We've coached a lot of people that were trying to exit or emotionally break free from toxic relationships. What has always been the most surprising is the fact that many people do not realize that they are in a toxic (and potentially abusive) relationship. Somewhere along the way, either within the current relationship or through their past relationship influences, they came to believe that struggle and hardship were normal for all relationships. That made it especially difficult to help them see what was and was not normal in relationships. This was their norm. Instead, it was more helpful for them to be able to see how much this relationship was negatively impacting their lives.

A toxic relationship is one that is consistently emotionally, physically, and mentally draining. While most traditional relationships have occasional rifts (usually resulting in growth), toxic relationships become an emotional torture chamber sending the victims on countless rollercoasters of anxiety, fear, shame, and self-conscious thought patterns. The impact assessment was all about helping you identify how much this relationship was dominating your life.

Take a few minutes to think about this. If you are in a place where you know that you were destined for more, or you can see how you've become a version of yourself that you don't recognize and you can trace some of the causes back to these relationships, what would you do to break free? How far would you go? What if all it took was you setting and committing to boundaries?

Establishing Boundaries Exercise: The Contact Management Plan

We've talked about establishing boundaries quite a bit and we know it was a lot to take in and think about. For some, boundaries may be new; for others, it might be something that you have tried but have been unsuccessful with setting (or keeping). This next exercise is all about preparing your mind for setting and keeping boundaries.

While you cannot always control or prevent when you'll come into contact with someone unwanted, your contact management plan will help you identify the times that you are likely to encounter those unwanted interactions. Then, we'll help you determine the best responses for those situations, as opposed to waiting until after they've baited you into a response. Each area of the contact management plan will have corresponding *Power Statements.*

Toxic people have the unique ability to make you feel out of control when you encounter them. Whether it's in person or over the phone, these interactions can bring on feelings of anxiety causing you to stutter, struggle to find your words, or for some, you can be flooded with uncontrollable emotions. Your *Power Statements* are short mantras that will give you the permission to take control of those situations-even if it's just to control you. You won't necessarily be verbalizing these statements while in conversation, but writing them down now gives you the opportunity to solidify your stance ahead of time.

The Contact Management Plan

1. What are the times that you are normally the *most* tempted to reach out to the person you are trying to detox from? Evenings? After you hear a certain song? After you've had a few drinks?

_____

My Power Statement:

Finish this statement: Reaching out to them would be betraying myself because . . .

_____

_____

2. Will there ever be an instance where I will *HAVE TO* (aka you have no choice but to) engage or correspond with my ex or anyone who is toxic to me? If yes, indicate why (Check all that apply below).

O Children (shared custody/visitation)

O Division of property

O Scheduling of legal/court appointments

O Physically live together so it's unavoidable

O Other (write it down) _____

_____

_____

The Contact Management Plan

My Power Statement:

Finish this statement: I will only engage or respond to them if . . .
Write down the ONLY circumstances where you will respond to or engage with them. This should be something that you can use to remind yourself what to do BEFORE you go down a path you regret. If it has nothing to do with these items you list here, do not engage.

_____

_____

_____

_____

Finish this statement: If it's not a predetermined topic, it's best I don't respond or engage because . . . (*What normally happens when you allow them to bait you into conversations or when you engage in unnecessary conversations? Are there things that happen that you usually regret when it's all said and done?*)

_____

_____

_____

_____

3. If I'm ever in contact with them and I begin to feel stressed or unsafe, I give myself permission to (choose as many as you like) . . .

- ⭕ Politely excuse myself from the situation or conversation.
- ⭕ Hang up on them.
- ⭕ Block them (permanently or temporarily until you're ready to try again).
- ⭕ Engage law enforcement if necessary.
- ⭕ Use a "contact management app" that will put space between me and them.

The Contact Management Plan

My Power Statement:

Create a statement that you can say to a person whenever you're engaged in a conversation that begins escalating to a place where you feel uncomfortable, afraid, or anxious. It will be used to give you back control and dictate your level of participation in the conversation once it reaches this point. Even if that level is zero participation. (**Example***: This conversation is no longer healthy or productive, so I'm ending it.)* Your turn. Create your power statement. Feel free to use or remix this one.

_____

_____

_____

_____

Finish this statement: If we share custody of children, I will limit all communication and responses to talking about . . . *Write down all the possible topics that you may need to discuss surrounding the kids (e.g. practices, pick-up/drop-off plans, school assignments, etc.).* Whatever it is, you're promising yourself that you will not engage with them if it does not have to do with these topics.

_____

_____

_____

_____

The Contact Management Plan

My Power Statement:

When the conversation begins to deviate from the list that you've created above, use this statement to either get the conversation back on track or excuse yourself from the conversation. (***Example***: *This conversation is supposed to be about [insert topic]. If you're not going to respect that, then I'm ending the conversation.*) Your turn. Create your power statement.

_____

_____

_____

_____

Adhering to this contact management plan will not be easy. Yes, you are scripting your responses in a sense. But what you're also doing is using this as a strategy to reprogram your brain for how you engage with toxic or healthy people, and creating a new habit for interacting with them. It will take practice, and you may even sound mechanical when saying these things to someone. The goal of this exercise is to give you a scripted process to follow during times where you typically become flustered or anxious. Resisting the temptation to go back to your "norm" is something that you must practice daily.

Step 2: The Flush (Purge)

Remove all gifts, novelties, keepsakes, and all other items that are associated with the person you're breaking soul-ties with. Yes, *everything*.

- Everything includes electronic keepsakes as well, like saved text messages, voice messages, or emails that remind you of who they used to be or how things started out. This keeps you holding out for hope. Take a deep breath and delete them. Try not to spend time reading over them again (even though we know you probably will).
- Box up everything to be either put away in storage, recycled, thrown away, or (when you're ready) sent back to the person who gave it to you.
- We don't necessarily recommend sending it back, because those situations have a likelihood to get emotional for you. For now, just put it away.

This step is going to be especially hard for those who are walking away from a romantic relationship. No matter how terrible that person treated us, and no matter how tragically the relationship ended, we have a habit of attaching ourselves to everything that the person came with, including the keepsakes and memorabilia exchanged during the relationship. The problem with attaching ourselves to the "things" from the relationship is that those "things" still keep us connected to them.

142

We understand that not *everything* about the relationship was bad. We get that some items or keepsakes carry a story or a sentimental connection. But as long as you're surrounded with pieces of them, you will never be able to be completely free of them. One look at the wrong thing has the ability to send you down a path of regret or shame. This process does not work if you're not prepared to completely let them go. So the purge is all about letting all the **stuff** go as well. This step is vitally important. Don't skip it.

TAKE A DEEP BREATH.
YOU CAN DO THIS.

Journal Exercises

What are the difficulties you are facing in starting this process? How are you feeling?

What do you think will be the most challenging part of flushing and fasting this week?

Imagine that your best friend is currently going through this process and has just hit the flush portion of their journey. What advice, support, or encouraging words would you give your best friend right now?

Set a reminder in your phone to tell you to read these encouraging words to yourself EVERY DAY until you no longer need it.

Prayer Journal

Write a prayer to help you through this phase of the journey. Revisit it as much as you need.

Your flush and fast will be continual throughout the rest of this journey. You'll constantly find things to get rid of, stop doing, or pack up. During this time, give yourself permission to grieve. Grieve the reality of the moment. Grieve the slow but sure disappearance of any signs of that person. Grieve every material that you pack up or throw away. Be real with it. Be present with it and grieve it all. Get clean inside and out.

Goodbye Letters Exercise———————————

Sure, you've already broken up with them and cut them off. And you have even managed to muster up the strength to block them. So you're probably confused by the need to write goodbye letters. Haven't we put you through enough? We have, but we promise there is a reason for this. And it's a good one.

It's likely that you either will or have already gone back and forth on your decision to completely let go of the people you are soul-tied to. Some of you have even gone back to the relationship, hoping for change, only to end up even more broken than you were to begin with. That's actually normal. It is hard to unlearn a habit, especially one that encompasses every part of your life or who you are.

This is why we compared this process to death. There are levels to this, and just because someone has died, it does not mean that you were ready or prepared to let them go. Just because their presence is no longer with you doesn't mean that your love for them went away with them. And when someone has not literally died, you will find yourself grieving and bargaining within your mind by trying to understand the things that you could have done differently or better. This is what typically sends you back into the arms of those who are no good for you—the idea that you can figure out what to do this time to make them be right for you. We get it. There is no shame or judgement in any teetering of your decisions right now.

Every part of this process takes a graduated step towards healing. Each phase will challenge you a little more than the one before. It will be difficult to complete this process if, with each step, you are not challenged to empty out your hope for the relationship that once was. Writing goodbye letters will be your proverbial obituary and your eulogy for the relationship. It will define who they were to you, announce that the relationship has ended, and put them (and the relationship that once was) to rest.

It's Time to Say Goodbye

This process is for you. Although you will write some things in your letters that you feel they *need* to hear, resist the temptation to send them these letters or to call them. If you feel you need to gain some sense of closure at the end of all this, consider mailing the letters to yourself, reading them out loud, and then literally burying the letters somewhere or burning them. The point of this is not the person you're breaking from. It's taking the time to articulate the finality of that relationship.

Who Do You Write To?

You are writing to the person or people that you are detoxing from. That includes but is not limited to:

- Exes
- Parents
- Siblings

- Other family
- Authority figures (i.e. spiritual leaders, teachers, coaches, mentors, bosses, etc.)
- Childhood or adolescent enemies and bullies
- Bad influences
- Someone you had an affair with

You're also writing a goodbye letter to intangible behaviors or inanimate things that you are detoxing from:

- Past behavior
- Habits
- Mentality or disposition
- Locations
- Events
- Employment
- Lifestyle
- Pain
- Brokenness
- Helplessness
- Powerlessness
- Coping mechanisms
- Etc.

When you're saying goodbye to those behaviors or habits, don't treat them as things going on inside of you. Treat them as if they are an entity or a person that exists outside of you. Call them by name, and then describe what they are. When you identify these habits or behaviors, you are not just saying goodbye. You are denouncing them as part of who you are.

Example of giving a behavior or habit a name:

"Dear Promiscuity (the fear that I cannot be loved unless I have sex with them)," **Or** "Dear Fear of Being Alone (that lie that tells me no one will want me unless I compromise myself or my standards)."

On the next page, we will give you a template to say goodbye. We'll provide five pages with the "Goodbye Letter Template" so that you can say goodbye to as many people and behaviors as you need. As you continue purging, and meditating on your journey to freedom, you may remember more people or behaviors that you need to say, "goodbye," to. Keep an additional journal handy for this. Releasing yourself from anyone or anything that is unhealthy for you will become part of your new norm.

Goodbye Letter Template

Dear [Person or Persona],

I am saying goodbye because . . .
[Write out all the reasons they are unhealthy for you, toxic to you, and why you must move on]

I know that if I stay . . .
[Write all the consequences that you know will happen if you continue to be in a relationship with them]

The blessing in saying goodbye is . . .
[Write out all the good things that you know will happen for you and you look forward to as a result of breaking bonds with them]

I'm moving on.

I release you and let you go.

Respectfully,

[Your Name]"

My Goodbye Letter to _____
(Name)

Dear _____

I am saying goodbye because . . .

I know that if I Stay....

The blessing in saying goodbye is...

I'm moving on.

I release you and let you go.

Respectfully,

_____
Sign and Date (so you never forget your first day of freedom)

My Goodbye Letter to _____
(Name)

Dear _____

I am saying goodbye because . . .

I know that if I Stay....

The blessing in saying goodbye is...

I'm moving on.

I release you and let you go.

Respectfully,

_____

Sign and Date (so you never forget your first day of freedom)

My Goodbye Letter to _____
(Name)

Dear _____

I am saying goodbye because . . .

I know that if I Stay....

The blessing in saying goodbye is...

I'm moving on.

I release you and let you go.

Respectfully,

_____

Sign and Date (so you never forget your first day of freedom)

My Goodbye Letter to _____

(Name)

Dear _____

I am saying goodbye because . . .

I know that if I Stay....

The blessing in saying goodbye is...

I'm moving on.

I release you and let you go.

Respectfully,

_____

Sign and Date (so you never forget your first day of freedom)

My Goodbye Letter to _____
(Name)

Dear _____

I am saying goodbye because . . .

I know that if I Stay....

The blessing in saying goodbye is...

I'm moving on.

I release you and let you go.

Respectfully,

_____
Sign and Date (so you never forget your first day of freedom)

Finalizing Your Goodbyes ───────────

Once you're done writing your letters, read them out loud to yourself. The say a prayer.

Thank God for His help in giving you the strength to move on.

Pray for His continued protection.

Pray for Him to grant you strength.

Pray for Him to direct you.

Pray for Him to be glorified in you.

Amen.

Small Group Discussion Questions

1. Earlier in phase three, the book talks about breaking the habit of certain people. How much of your attachment to that person or those people actually feels like a habit to you? Have you ever considered your relationships like this before?

2. Is there anyone that you "cut off" that you will need extra support or accountability to help you stay away from them?

3. When it came to removing the catalysts around you, was there anything that you either refused to remove from your environment or that you had an extremely hard time removing?

4. Do you think cleansing your environment will help you move forward?

5. How many people did you write goodbye letters to? Which was the hardest to write?

This is the end of week two. Please take time to review, complete your work for this week, and continue to cleanse your physical, mental, and emotional spaces.

WEEKS THREE AND FOUR

PHASE FOUR

FACING THE ENEMY

Do not fret because of those who are evil or be envious of those who do wrong; 2 for like the grass they will soon wither, like green plants they will soon die away. 3 Trust in the Lord and do good; dwell in the land and enjoy safe pasture. 4 Take delight in the Lord, and he will give you the desires of your heart. **Psalm 37:1-4 (NIV)**

Phase Four: Facing the Enemy

As you enter this week, we want to remind you to continue the work from the previous week. Continue purging your physical environment of those things that keep you in connection with those you want to break free from. You will be surprised at the random items that may come up and spark memories for you—good or bad. In order to keep moving forward, discard them or pack them away as soon as you see them. We don't want anything contaminating your progress.

It is also important that this does not become a dreaded process of grief and throwing things away. Challenge yourself to go beyond the purging and develop a mindset that inspires a sense of renewal and refreshing. Consider activities like rearranging furniture, painting walls, purchasing new décor, or even buying new clothes. All these activities invite a sense of new beginning and will empower you to take control of your feelings and your environment. With activities like this, you are making definitive decisions about you and your atmosphere without considering anyone else. Believe it or not, refreshing is a part of the purge that has to be practiced more than anything else. You have to intentionally practice being your authentic self without considering those who have influenced your thoughts or behaviors for so long. It can be liberating and scary all at the same time.

You're Not the Only One With The Soul-Tie ————

While you may be the one dodging calls, texts, and messages from whoever you're releasing, they are struggling because your absence is becoming more and more apparent. Where there once was an abundance of control and influence over you, they now feel you slipping away from their grip. A lot of times we have people that will complain that their ex or toxic people won't stop calling them, or they're playing mind games with their love and affection. This is because, just as you are trying to break free from them, they're desperately trying to maintain a position of influence over you. Remember, we are talking about habits. You're their habit as much as they were yours. So even if they don't have the words to articulate what they are doing, they are still the antagonist to your healing right now, and you need to protect yourself from their attempts. Stay vigilant with your boundaries and adjust them (or escalate them) if necessary.

Weeks three and four are going to be pivotal for you. During this time, you will be challenged to face your enemies. Last week we focused on the physical removal of the person (or people) you are disconnecting from. This next phase will be about the mental and emotional confrontation of them. You will not just be facing your wounds, you will be examining the cause of those wounds. You will be challenged to acknowledge and admit who your enemies actually are, and it won't always be apparent. We will caution you in advance that this will not be easy.

Acknowledging Your Enemy ————

Whenever someone goes through an addiction treatment program, they are often surprised by the level of "safeguards" that are required in order to be successful in the program. At the onset, these safeguards feel like a restrictive prison. What is later discovered is that there were several people, places, and behaviors that seemed harmless, but were actually contributing to their habit. Once they were able to look at their environments with clarity, they could recognize everything and everyone that had become an enemy to their recovery.

The hardest part of this aspect of recovery was coming to terms with the idea that people who they loved and trusted were actually enemies of their progress. It's easy to identify an enemy that is functioning in an antagonistic way. But when those enemies are covert, or people we have a familial obligation to, it's much harder than it seems to actually see them for who they are and call them by name.

These two weeks of mental and emotional cleansing will require you to be honest about your enemies. It takes two weeks because it's a lot of work. You're going to revisit some hurts and you'll have to be honest about not just who caused those hurts, but the impact of those hurts as well. Some will be from your childhood, others will be more recent. What will become very clear during this time is the number of hurts you have suppressed or overlooked over time, and the number of people who have never been held accountable for their role in your hurt. Even if you never address them, you will have to acknowledge them in order to move forward.

This will be the only time that we will ask you to look back into your past and bring up negative memories. So take your time and be as thorough as possible. We want to give you the room and the space to feel the anger, frustration, embarrassment, hurt, shame, guilt, sadness, neglect, abandonment, betrayal, and abuse. By facing these feelings, and assigning accountability, you're going to unearth every rotting corpse in the grave of your past and prepare them for burial.

You will need to find alone time during this part of the process—a place for free, uninhibited emotional expression as you document the incidents and injuries of your enemies. There may be times where you will want to cry out loud. There may be instances where you want to yell or scream into a pillow. Whatever your emotional response is or may be, we will want you to give yourself personal space to express it without restraint and without interruption.

Facing The Enemies From Your Youth ——————

Our developmental years are usually when we cultivate our perception of love and our tolerance for pain. From how we interact with our peers and loved ones to how we acclimate socially, our entire worldview is being developed from these childhood experiences. Some experiences from our youth may be blurred. Others may be neatly tucked away because we never believed them to be a big deal. But more often than not, our childhood experiences have a habit of developing sleeper cells of pain in the dark corners of our minds. Those pains then become catalysts for grownup habits and behaviors.

As you're going through this exercise, we want you to be honest about things that have hurt you, but we don't want you to force experiences to be painful either. Some hurts will be inconsequential, and that's okay. There may be others that are catastrophic. The point of this exercise will be to recognize the significant pain from your past and the enemies responsible and to identify how these events have informed your adult habits. Then you will properly lay your pain to rest.

Facing Your Guardian Enemies

Parents, guardians, and authority figures can all be considered under this category—those who were entrusted with our lives during our youth and who we had no choice but to trust. From tiny infants to blossoming adolescents, we depend on our parents and authority figures to design our view of the world. They have the power to prepare us for life by building us up or breaking us down, to awaken the kings and queens in us or create slaves to fear. And if they abandon their responsibility to build us up, so much inside of us breaks that it makes it difficult to know what healthy love is supposed to look like.

We have all been shaped by those who raised us. If we've been hurt by our authority figures, it has the ability to steal pieces of our lives from us without us even recognizing it. Growing up in environments where there was rejection, abandonment, control, or abuse has a way of distorting our view of love and how we view ourselves. Whether it's out of fear, respect, or a cultural code of honor, these wounds are allowed to lay dormant because we are expected to remain silent. And because of their position (in our family or in title), we tend to excuse their behavior as if they are above humanity. But they are human. If you allow their role in life to keep you from acknowledging their failure, then the unidentified pain of your past will wreak havoc on your future.

You are about to face the enemies of your past. There are so many ways that you could have been hurt by those bigger than you. It doesn't have to be deep or catastrophic to matter. There is nothing too small or too trivial to write about. If it has caused you pain, then it is valid. Write about it.

This part of the process will likely be the most challenging so we don't want you to rush through it. This is why we've provided for two weeks for this phase. Take your time to complete all of the assignments and take necessary breaks in between.

Journal Exercise
Facing Your Guardian Enemies

In this exercise, you're going to take time to write out the answers to the following questions in your journal. There can be more than one person in this category that hurt you, so repeat this exercise as many times as necessary for each person involved. We'll give you enough space to answer the questions for at least five people but, if you find that you need to list more people in this category, we recommend having an additional journal handy.

Facing Your Guardian Enemies

1. Who hurt you (Their name and title)? Note: Title is mother, father, uncle, aunt, pastor, sitter, etc.

2. How did they hurt you? – i.e. [name/title] hurt me when . . .

3. How did this make you feel? Be as descriptive as you can or need.

4. How do you think this experience affects your habits or patterns today?

- Are you constantly afraid of being abandoned by people you love?
- Has that caused you to campaign to prove yourself in relationships? Or is it the opposite in that you let go of people too easily?
- Do you have trust issues? Do you fear that people aren't who they're supposed to be?
- Because you weren't loved right, do you feel unworthy of love or like no one will ever love you?
- Because you're not used to closeness, does the idea of intimacy scare you?
- Due to feeling unloved, are you constantly trying to prove your worth in a relationship?

Write about it.

5. Before now, have you ever been able to acknowledge these wounds and assign accountability for them? Write about how you are going to move forward in life after acknowledging them within this process (Whether your answer is yes or no).

Facing Your Guardian Enemies

1. Who hurt you (Their name and title)? Note: Title is mother, father, uncle, aunt, pastor, sitter, etc.

2. How did they hurt you? – i.e. [name/title] hurt me when . . .

3. How did this make you feel? Be as descriptive as you can or need.

4. How do you think this experience affects your habits or patterns today?
- Are you constantly afraid of being abandoned by people you love?
- Has that caused you to campaign to prove yourself in relationships? Or is it the opposite in that you let go of people too easily?
- Do you have trust issues? Do you fear that people aren't who they're supposed to be?
- Because you weren't loved right, do you feel unworthy of love or like no one will ever love you?
- Because you're not used to closeness, does the idea of intimacy scare you?
- Due to feeling unloved, are you constantly trying to prove your worth in a relationship?

Write about it.

5. Before now, have you ever been able to acknowledge these wounds and assign accountability for them? Write about how you are going to move forward in life after acknowledging them within this process (Whether your answer is yes or no).

Facing Your Guardian Enemies

1. Who hurt you (Their name and title)? Note: Title is mother, father, uncle, aunt, pastor, sitter, etc.

2. How did they hurt you? – i.e. [name/title] hurt me when . . .

3. How did this make you feel? Be as descriptive as you can or need.

4. How do you think this experience affects your habits or patterns today?
- Are you constantly afraid of being abandoned by people you love?
- Has that caused you to campaign to prove yourself in relationships? Or is it the opposite in that you let go of people too easily?
- Do you have trust issues? Do you fear that people aren't who they're supposed to be?
- Because you weren't loved right, do you feel unworthy of love or like no one will ever love you?
- Because you're not used to closeness, does the idea of intimacy scare you?
- Due to feeling unloved, are you constantly trying to prove your worth in a relationship?

Write about it.

5. Before now, have you ever been able to acknowledge these wounds and assign accountability for them? Write about how you are going to move forward in life after acknowledging them within this process (Whether your answer is yes or no).

Facing Your Guardian Enemies

1. Who hurt you (Their name and title)? Note: Title is mother, father, uncle, aunt, pastor, sitter, etc.

2. How did they hurt you? – i.e. [name/title] hurt me when . . .

3. How did this make you feel? Be as descriptive as you can or need.

4. How do you think this experience affects your habits or patterns today?

- Are you constantly afraid of being abandoned by people you love?
- Has that caused you to campaign to prove yourself in relationships? Or is it the opposite in that you let go of people too easily?
- Do you have trust issues? Do you fear that people aren't who they're supposed to be?
- Because you weren't loved right, do you feel unworthy of love or like no one will ever love you?
- Because you're not used to closeness, does the idea of intimacy scare you?
- Due to feeling unloved, are you constantly trying to prove your worth in a relationship?

Write about it.

5. Before now, have you ever been able to acknowledge these wounds and assign accountability for them? Write about how you are going to move forward in life after acknowledging them within this process (Whether your answer is yes or no).

Facing Your Guardian Enemies

1. Who hurt you (Their name and title)? Note: Title is mother, father, uncle, aunt, pastor, sitter, etc.

2. How did they hurt you? – i.e. [name/title] hurt me when . . .

3. How did this make you feel? Be as descriptive as you can or need.

4. How do you think this experience affects your habits or patterns today?
- Are you constantly afraid of being abandoned by people you love?
- Has that caused you to campaign to prove yourself in relationships? Or is it the opposite in that you let go of people too easily?
- Do you have trust issues? Do you fear that people aren't who they're supposed to be?
- Because you weren't loved right, do you feel unworthy of love or like no one will ever love you?
- Because you're not used to closeness, does the idea of intimacy scare you?
- Due to feeling unloved, are you constantly trying to prove your worth in a relationship?

Write about it.

5. Before now, have you ever been able to acknowledge these wounds and assign accountability for them? Write about how you are going to move forward in life after acknowledging them within this process (Whether your answer is yes or no).

In these exercises, it's important to understand that their behavior was not a statement about you, it was a statement about them. You didn't fail as a child, they failed you as an adult.

The Action

For each adult that you identified in this exercise, write out the following statement:

"[Their name] hurt me when they [summarize what they did]. Their behavior and treatment towards me was not ok. They failed me and as a result, it has hurt me. As I move forward, I will hold them accountable for the pain they have caused. But I will no longer allow what they did to negatively impact my life.

This detox is the first step of reclaiming my life.

There are five blank templates of this declaration in case you need to assign accountability to more than one person.

Declaration

_____

(Their Name)

hurt me when they

_____

_____

_____

_____

Their behavior and treatment towards me was not ok. They failed me and as a result, it has hurt me. As I move forward, I will hold them accountable for the pain they have caused. But I will no longer allow what they did to negatively impact my life.

This detox is the first step of reclaiming my life.

_____

Sign and Date

Declaration

_____

(Their Name)

hurt me when they

_____

_____

_____

_____

Their behavior and treatment towards me was not ok. They failed me and as a result, it has hurt me. As I move forward, I will hold them accountable for the pain they have caused. But I will no longer allow what they did to negatively impact my life.

This detox is the first step of reclaiming my life.

_____

Sign and Date

Declaration

_____

(Their Name)

hurt me when they

_____

_____

_____

_____

Their behavior and treatment towards me was not ok. They failed me and as a result, it has hurt me. As I move forward, I will hold them accountable for the pain they have caused. But I will no longer allow what they did to negatively impact my life.

This detox is the first step of reclaiming my life.

_____

Sign and Date

Declaration

_____

(Their Name)

hurt me when they

_____

_____

_____

_____

Their behavior and treatment towards me was not ok. They failed me and as a result, it has hurt me. As I move forward, I will hold them accountable for the pain they have caused. But I will no longer allow what they did to negatively impact my life.

This detox is the first step of reclaiming my life.

_____

Sign and Date

Declaration

_____

(Their Name)

hurt me when they

_____

_____

_____

_____

Their behavior and treatment towards me was not ok. They failed me and as a result, it has hurt me. As I move forward, I will hold them accountable for the pain they have caused. But I will no longer allow what they did to negatively impact my life.

This detox is the first step of reclaiming my life.

_____

Sign and Date

This exercise is not just about dredging up pain from your past. It's about connecting these past pain points to identify present influences. Once you can freely and honestly connect the dots of your past to your present, you can begin the process of charting a new path for your future. Depending on the depth of the hurt you just wrote about, we will always advise you to consider additional resources like counseling. Some pains are too heavy to unpack here, so we want you to be mindful of how these memories may be adversely affecting you. If you find that these memories are impacting your ability to function from day to day, seek a therapist that specializes in trauma. Don't be afraid to get the help that you need.

Enemies of Your Youth: Your Childhood Peers

As a little girl growing up in the "hood" of San Bernardino, California, I always felt out of place. My mom and step-dad drove the church van (so it stayed parked in our yard), we could never play with other kids in our neighborhood, and our mother always used to remind us that just because we lived in the ghetto didn't mean we had to act like it. So we were taught to speak well, mind our elders, and avoid trouble. I was called an Oreo (black on the outside, white on the inside) and a white girl my entire childhood life. I was bullied for not being able to afford nice clothes and shoes and teased for never going to parties. And everyone always told me that my expectations of life outside of the ghetto were unrealistic. It wasn't until we started writing this book that I realized how much this impacted me.

I have spent a great deal of my adult life working to prove those people wrong. Mix in some daddy issues, and your girl was a mess. For the longest time, I had various voices in my head reminding me of what everyone said I would not be, and it caused me to work harder—to the point of exhaustion. After acknowledging this, I had to reevaluate the "why" behind so much of my drive and reassign my value to something that wasn't attached to what others had caused me to believe about myself.

As children, we spent an enormous amount of time with our peers. Through our experiences with our peers, we developed socially, adapted to ideas of social hierarchy, and discovered things that our guardians didn't show us or teach us. We were vulnerable to our peers. For the most part, our experiences were pleasant. However, it is around this time in our lives that we might encounter bullying, ostracizing, embarrassments, or even suffer from abuse of some sort. Hurt experienced during our childhood, especially from our peers, can play a factor in our adult lives and decisions.

Take a moment and answer the following questions in your journal again. Since there could have been more than one person in this category that hurt you, repeat as many times as necessary for each person involved.

Facing The Enemy in Your Childhood Peers

1. Who hurt you (Their name and title)? Note: Title includes friend, classmate, crush, cousin, etc.

2. How did they hurt you? – i.e. [name/title] hurt me when . . .

3. How did this make you feel? Be as descriptive as you can or need.

4. How do you think this experience affects your habits or patterns today?
- Are you constantly afraid of being abandoned by people you love?
- Has that caused you to campaign to prove yourself in relationships? Or is it the opposite in that you let go of people too easily?
- Do you have trust issues? Do you fear that people aren't who they're supposed to be?
- Because you weren't loved right, do you feel unworthy of love or like no one will ever love you?
- Because you're not used to closeness, does the idea of intimacy scare you?
- Due to feeling unloved, are you constantly trying to prove your worth in a relationship?

Write about it.

5. Before now, have you ever been able to acknowledge these wounds and assign accountability for them? Write about how you are going to move forward in life after acknowledging them within this process (Whether your answer is yes or no).

Facing The Enemy in Your Childhood Peers

1. Who hurt you (Their name and title)? Note: Title includes friend, classmate, crush, cousin, etc.

2. How did they hurt you? – i.e. [name/title] hurt me when . . .

3. How did this make you feel? Be as descriptive as you can or need.

4. How do you think this experience affects your habits or patterns today?
- Are you constantly afraid of being abandoned by people you love?
- Has that caused you to campaign to prove yourself in relationships? Or is it the opposite in that you let go of people too easily?
- Do you have trust issues? Do you fear that people aren't who they're supposed to be?
- Because you weren't loved right, do you feel unworthy of love or like no one will ever love you?
- Because you're not used to closeness, does the idea of intimacy scare you?
- Due to feeling unloved, are you constantly trying to prove your worth in a relationship?

Write about it.

5. Before now, have you ever been able to acknowledge these wounds and assign accountability for them? Write about how you are going to move forward in life after acknowledging them within this process (Whether your answer is yes or no).

Facing The Enemy in Your Childhood Peers

1. Who hurt you (Their name and title)? Note: Title includes friend, classmate, crush, cousin, etc.

2. How did they hurt you? – i.e. [name/title] hurt me when . . .

3. How did this make you feel? Be as descriptive as you can or need.

4. How do you think this experience affects your habits or patterns today?
- Are you constantly afraid of being abandoned by people you love?
- Has that caused you to campaign to prove yourself in relationships? Or is it the opposite in that you let go of people too easily?
- Do you have trust issues? Do you fear that people aren't who they're supposed to be?
- Because you weren't loved right, do you feel unworthy of love or like no one will ever love you?
- Because you're not used to closeness, does the idea of intimacy scare you?
- Due to feeling unloved, are you constantly trying to prove your worth in a relationship?

Write about it.

5. Before now, have you ever been able to acknowledge these wounds and assign accountability for them? Write about how you are going to move forward in life after acknowledging them within this process (Whether your answer is yes or no).

Facing The Enemy in Your Childhood Peers

1. Who hurt you (Their name and title)? Note: Title includes friend, classmate, crush, cousin, etc.

2. How did they hurt you? – i.e. [name/title] hurt me when . . .

3. How did this make you feel? Be as descriptive as you can or need.

4. How do you think this experience affects your habits or patterns today?
- Are you constantly afraid of being abandoned by people you love?
- Has that caused you to campaign to prove yourself in relationships? Or is it the opposite in that you let go of people too easily?
- Do you have trust issues? Do you fear that people aren't who they're supposed to be?
- Because you weren't loved right, do you feel unworthy of love or like no one will ever love you?
- Because you're not used to closeness, does the idea of intimacy scare you?
- Due to feeling unloved, are you constantly trying to prove your worth in a relationship?

Write about it.

5. Before now, have you ever been able to acknowledge these wounds and assign accountability for them? Write about how you are going to move forward in life after acknowledging them within this process (Whether your answer is yes or no).

Facing The Enemy in Your Childhood Peers

1. Who hurt you (Their name and title)? Note: Title includes friend, classmate, crush, cousin, etc.

2. How did they hurt you? – i.e. [name/title] hurt me when . . .

3. How did this make you feel? Be as descriptive as you can or need.

4. How do you think this experience affects your habits or patterns today?
- Are you constantly afraid of being abandoned by people you love?
- Has that caused you to campaign to prove yourself in relationships? Or is it the opposite in that you let go of people too easily?
- Do you have trust issues? Do you fear that people aren't who they're supposed to be?
- Because you weren't loved right, do you feel unworthy of love or like no one will ever love you?
- Because you're not used to closeness, does the idea of intimacy scare you?
- Due to feeling unloved, are you constantly trying to prove your worth in a relationship?

Write about it.

5. Before now, have you ever been able to acknowledge these wounds and assign accountability for them? Write about how you are going to move forward in life after acknowledging them within this process (Whether your answer is yes or no).

Their behavior was not a statement about you, it was a statement about them. You didn't fail as a child. They failed you, and whoever molded them failed you.

The Action

For each peer that you identified in this exercise, write out the following statement:

"[Their name] hurt me when they [summarize what they did]. Their behavior and treatment towards me was not ok. They failed me and as a result, it has hurt me. As I move forward, I will hold them accountable for the pain they have caused. But I will no longer allow what they did to negatively impact my life.

This detox is the first step of reclaiming my life.

There are five blank templates of this declaration in case you need to assign accountability to more than one person.

Declaration

_____

(Their Name)

hurt me when they

_____

_____

_____

_____

Their behavior and treatment towards me was not ok. They failed me and as a result, it has hurt me. As I move forward, I will hold them accountable for the pain they have caused. But I will no longer allow what they did to negatively impact my life.

This detox is the first step of reclaiming my life.

_____

Sign and Date

Declaration

_____
(Their Name)

hurt me when they
_____
_____
_____
_____

Their behavior and treatment towards me was not ok. They failed me and as a result, it has hurt me. As I move forward, I will hold them accountable for the pain they have caused. But I will no longer allow what they did to negatively impact my life.

This detox is the first step of reclaiming my life.

_____
Sign and Date

Declaration

_____

(Their Name)

hurt me when they

_____

_____

_____

_____

Their behavior and treatment towards me was not ok. They failed me and as a result, it has hurt me. As I move forward, I will hold them accountable for the pain they have caused. But I will no longer allow what they did to negatively impact my life.

This detox is the first step of reclaiming my life.

_____

Sign and Date

Declaration

_____

(Their Name)

hur me when they

_____

_____

_____

_____

Their behavior and treatment towards me was not ok. They failed me and as a result, it has hurt me. As I move forward, I will hold them accountable for the pain they have caused. But I will no longer allow what they did to negatively impact my life.

This detox is the first step of reclaiming my life.

_____

Sign and Date

Declaration

_____

(Their Name)

hurt me when they

_____

_____

_____

_____

Their behavior and treatment towards me was not ok. They failed me and as a result, it has hurt me. As I move forward, I will hold them accountable for the pain they have caused. But I will no longer allow what they did to negatively impact my life.

This detox is the first step of reclaiming my life.

_____

Sign and Date

Facing Your Exes

The emotional place that you're in right now is torture. You love them and you're certain that they love you too. You've fought hard to hold onto them and the relationship, but deep down you know that they are unsafe for you. Yet and still, trying to convince you to stop fighting for your love, or to stop praying for a miracle, feels impossible. This is the point that it becomes torture. Even though you serve a God who can do the impossible, you have to contend with the fact that He won't force someone to change or to love you the way you deserve. They have to want to change. And your heart breaks a little bit more because you have to force yourself to see that they would have changed already, if they wanted to.

During these times, it's easy to subconsciously separate their faults, idiosyncrasies, and toxicity from them as a person. You become convinced that they act the way they do because they are a victim of something or someone else. Whether they had an abusive childhood, had a traumatic experience, or even they themselves had a bad relationship, it's easier to love them through their toxicity when there is an explanation outside of them. And regardless of how much you've already suffered and sacrificed, you still feel an overwhelming sense of guilt because it feels like you're giving up on them, like you didn't try hard enough to love them before giving up. This guilt, this defeat that you're feeling, is what has kept you from truly acknowledging who your ex really is. It is what will continue to keep you broken until you face it.

So let's just say it once and for all. This is who they are. Whatever explanation exists for their behavior, it's not justification for that behavior. You've seen the behavior, you've lived through one too many broken promises, and you've been on this roller coaster of emotions for far too long. When their behavior consistently contradicts their words, they are incapable of protecting your heart and keeping you safe. And while it absolutely takes two people to build or break a relationship, it only takes one person to make selfish and bad choices to break the other person in that relationship. You are not nor have you ever been responsible for them or their actions. Their choices are their burden. And if their choices hurt you, give yourself permission to remove yourself as a consequence.

It's time to face it all and call your transgressor by name. In this next exercise, you will write out all the ways that they have *chosen* to hurt you and acknowledge why they are no longer safe for you.

Write out the full sentences and answer the following questions as detailed as you can within your journal. If you will be "facing" more than one ex in this exercise, repeat these sentences and write out these exercises as many times as you need to. We've left space for you to complete three within the book.

Facing Your Exes

1. Who hurt you (Their name)?

2. How did they hurt you? – i.e. [name] hurt me when . . .

3. How did your relationship with them change you? *How did it affect how you saw yourself? Did it impact your confidence or self-esteem? Did you become a version of yourself that you didn't recognize? Write it out.*

4. Even though you miss them and wish they would change, what aspects of the relationship (or them) will you **not** miss? *Think about the things that gave you anxiety, made you second-guess yourself, or hurt your feelings. Be descriptive.*

5. What toxic tendencies, if any, did you develop as a result of that relationship?

6. Do they have influence over you (are you in any way weak to them)? *As a result of their influence, what sort of things have you done in the relationship that you later regretted? Why is it time that you break their influence over you?*

7. Why is this person no longer safe for you? Why is a relationship with this person bad for you?

Facing Your Exes

1. Who hurt you (Their name)?

2. How did they hurt you? – i.e. [name] hurt me when . . .

3. How did your relationship with them change you? *How did it affect how you saw yourself? Did it impact your confidence or self-esteem? Did you become a version of yourself that you didn't recognize? Write it out.*

4. Even though you miss them and wish they would change, what aspects of the relationship (or them) will you **not** miss? *Think about the things that gave you anxiety, made you second-guess yourself, or hurt your feelings. Be descriptive.*

5. What toxic tendencies, if any, did you develop as a result of that relationship?

6. Do they have influence over you (are you in any way weak to them)? *As a result of their influence, what sort of things have you done in the relationship that you later regretted? Why is it time that you break their influence over you?*

7. Why is this person no longer safe for you? Why is a relationship with this person bad for you?

Facing Your Exes

1. Who hurt you (Their name)?

2. How did they hurt you? – i.e. [name] hurt me when . . .

3. How did your relationship with them change you? *How did it affect how you saw yourself? Did it impact your confidence or self-esteem? Did you become a version of yourself that you didn't recognize? Write it out.*

4. Even though you miss them and wish they would change, what aspects of the relationship (or them) will you **not** miss? *Think about the things that gave you anxiety, made you second-guess yourself, or hurt your feelings. Be descriptive.*

5. What toxic tendencies, if any, did you develop as a result of that relationship?

6. Do they have influence over you (are you in any way weak to them)? *As a result of their influence, what sort of things have you done in the relationship that you later regretted? Why is it time that you break their influence over you?*

7. Why is this person no longer safe for you? Why is a relationship with this person bad for you?

Week Four Begins Here

This is the beginning of a new day for you. This purging process will help to finally disconnect from those pains that may have adversely affected you.

Facing the Enemy in Me ───────────

One of the greatest benefits we have as adults is our ability to make our own decisions. While our decisions may be colored by our past experiences, everything still boils down to a choice. The beauty and the burden of this fact is that our choices give us the opportunity to either break the cycles that were developed in our youth or perpetuate them. The purpose of "Facing the Enemy" in this entire process has been about leading you to this place. It's about helping you see how the enemies of your past have shaped you and giving you the opportunity to make new choices based on that information.

It will be impossible to walk in the fullness of freedom without taking accountability for our past choices, including our failures. It's important to understand that this is not an exercise of victim-blaming. You are not at fault for someone else's choices to hurt you. This will be about honestly evaluating choices that you've made where you were in complete control and had the opportunity to choose differently.

- Were you too passive?
- Could you have walked away earlier?
- Did you not pay attention to the red flags?
- Perhaps you saw the flags and ignored them.

- Maybe you thought the person would change or that you could change them.
- Maybe you settled and didn't love yourself first.
- Maybe you tolerated behavior or treatment that you didn't have to tolerate because of fear.

There are so many reasons why you could have made the decisions you've made. Some reasons could be honorable in nature, while others could be mean and spiteful. The reason that you have to come to terms with your choices is to set a precedent in the timeline of your life. You're giving yourself the opportunity to look back at key moments in your life, identifying the choices that impacted those moments, and then seeing the result of your choices and how they impacted your life. When you're honest enough to admit you had choices in these moments, you empower yourself to have different choices moving forward. This is where you will draw a line of demarcation that doesn't ignore your past mistakes but gives you permission to become a new version of you that makes different, better choices. This is what we mean by facing the enemy within you.

The series of questions in this next section will use past relationships as a mirror in order to see yourself. This is the part in your journal where you get emotionally naked, stand in the mirror, and get real. Don't tear yourself down. Just be honest about who you've been.

Take some time and answer the following questions in your journal. We'll guide this activity through our prompts and questions. Remember to see yourself from the perspective of a relationship you've had.

FACING THE ENEMY IN ME:
Before Your Most-Recent
Intimate Relationship

These questions focus on your most recent romantic relationship. Your toxic soul-tie may not be with someone that you were intimately involved with; however, intimate partners can serve as great mirrors since they were people we were the most vulnerable with. These questions will help you to see yourself through those mirrors.

1. Take a look at who you were *before* your last intimate relationship. Where were you in life? Be descriptive. Include where you were living, working, going to school, etc.

2. What could you have done differently to prepare yourself for a relationship?

Examples of what others have said they would have done differently:

- Spent more time getting to know and falling in love with myself.
- Been more patient with myself and the dating process so I didn't rush into relationships.
- Learned to date in a way that honors my love language but guards my heart.
- Learned to not let external pressures inform my decisions.
- Learned how to walk away without allowing guilt or shame to paralyze me.

Write about it.

3. Based on the things you could have done differently to prepare for relationships, why would this preparation have been helpful?

4. How will you address this in yourself so you can be different in future relationships?

FACING THE ENEMY IN ME:
In the **Beginning** of Your Most-
Recent Intimate Relationship

These questions will focus the early part of your most recent romantic relationship. That "honeymoon" period where you were so into them that it seemed like nothing else mattered.

1. Take yourself back to the beginning of your most recent intimate relationship where everything was new and exciting. Was there anything you could have done differently before falling too deep? If yes, what was it and how would it have been helpful to you?

2. Were there any behaviors or red flags that you missed or ignored? If yes, what do you wish you would have done when you first noticed these red flags?

3. If there were any red flags that you ignored, why do you think you overlooked them?

4. What needs to change in you to prevent you from making these same mistakes in future relationships?

FACING THE ENEMY IN ME:
During Your Most-Recent
Intimate Relationship

Now we are going to take a look at the time after you've settled into your relationship with them.

---

1. Were there any mistakes or lapses in judgement that you saw yourself making in the relationship? If yes, how did these mistakes impact or change the relationship? If yes, list them.

---

2. Were there moments in your most recent relationship where you said things that you shouldn't have said? Was there a pattern of speaking in a way that was harmful or damaging in nature (regardless of your reasoning)? If yes, describe those behaviors.

3. Were there things in your most recent relationship that you tolerated that you know you shouldn't have? List the things you tolerated.

4. Why do you think that you tolerated this behavior that you know you shouldn't have? What do you think would have happened if you didn't tolerate this behavior?

5. What, if anything, do you need to do in order to develop into a person that does not tolerate this kind of behavior?

——————————————————— ℓℓ ———————————————————

6. Did you find that you neglected yourself to please others?

○ Yes   ○ No

> How could putting yourself first have benefited you more in the relationship?

7. Were you ever too aggressive in the relationship (about your needs, demands, or desires)?

○ Yes   ○ No

> If so, what were some of the most common responses to your aggressiveness in the relationship?

8. In your most recent relationship, did you try to change anything about them that you originally accepted?

○ Yes   ○ No

> If so, how would your relationship have been different if you did not try to change anything about them (or think that you could change anything)?

9. Of all these "behaviors" that you were able to relate to or identify with, were there any that you could recognize as a pattern within your other relationships (family, friends, or intimate relationships)? Take a moment to review this list and reflect on all of your other relationships. If you notice any patterns of behavior, write those patterns out and identify what other relationships you've noticed this pattern with.

Weeks Three + Four

10. Now that you've had a chance to review any past mistakes you've made in relationships, what do you need to change within you to avoid these same mistakes in the future? What are you committed to doing to help you unlearn these patterns and habits?
Take your time here.

Weeks Three + Four

Take a breath. You should be proud of yourself. It takes courage to admit when you're wrong. It takes strength to identify times within intimate relationships that you could've done something differently, especially when it's within relationships where you have been hurt. But doing things differently becomes easier when you commit to thinking differently about yourself.

If you find that you need additional resources like counseling or coaching to help you unlearn habits and behaviors, by all means get help. It's never too late to begin again.

Toxic Tendencies

Let's be honest here. Everything that happened in your toxic relationship with your ex wasn't always their fault. They are absolutely responsible for their choices, but they may not have been the only toxic participant in the relationship. Coming out of a relationship where there has been toxicity or abuse, it's easy to place all of the responsibility on the person who caused us harm. However, if there are never attempts to identify the toxic tendencies that facilitated the toxicity or abuse, it is easy for the past to be repeated with someone else. At every juncture in life, it is important to take an honest look at yourself to ensure you are learning and unlearning the things that do or do not serve you.

We all have our own toxic traits that we bring into our relationships. They're the decisions we've made, the mentalities that we've functioned within, and the perspectives we've always approached life from. And because these tendencies have been a part of our norm and connected to who we are, it can be challenging to identify them as being toxic. Yes, you can have toxic tendencies and not even realize it. That's why it is so important for us to address. It would do you no good to heal from everything that has happened to you without addressing any dysfunction within you. Identifying your own toxic traits, and committing to doing the work of unlearning them, will prevent you from carrying them from one relationship to the next.

Toxic Tendencies Worksheet

—— ℘ ——

We've created the list below to help you identify any traits that you may have, or traits that you have but may not be aware are toxic. This is not an exhaustive list of toxic tendencies, but these are the most common and some of the most important to use for self-reflection.

It's Time To Dig … DEEP.

If you are unsure about any of these, have a problem answering any of these questions, or have trouble recognizing any of these in you, ask a friend or family member to work through this with you. Be sure it's someone who knows you and is willing to be honest about their experiences with you—someone that is invested in your continued growth. *It's not wise to ask the person you're breaking the soul-tie with or an ex.*

Do You Require Instant Gratification? (check any that apply to you)

1. Are you impatient? ⭕ YES ⭕ NO

2. Are you usually in a rush to get what you want? ⭕ YES ⭕ NO

3. Do you get upset when something doesn't go your way as fast as you need it to? ⭕ YES ⭕ NO

4. Have you found yourself in trouble or regretting decisions in relationships because you rushed into it? ⭕ YES ⭕ NO

Toxic Tendencies Worksheet

Do You Chase Relationship Highs? (check any that apply to you)

1. Do you chase people or relationships like chasing a high? ⭕ YES ⭕ NO

2. Is your favorite part of a relationship the beginning? ⭕ YES ⭕ NO

3. When the "honeymoon" phase is over in a relationship, do you panic from fear that the relationship is dead? ⭕ YES ⭕ NO

4. Do you get bored or lose interest easily in relationships? ⭕ YES ⭕ NO

5. Do you panic when relationships experience "bumps" or arguments? ⭕ YES ⭕ NO

6. Do you do everything in your power to avoid relationship turmoil or "bumps in the road?" ⭕ YES ⭕ NO

Toxic Tendencies Worksheet

Are You Comfortable in Dishonesty? (check any that apply to you)

1. Is it easy for you to be dishonest in your relationships? O YES O NO

2. Do you believe it's okay to hide or withhold information? O YES O NO

3. Have you ever justified the idea of "what they don't know can't hurt them"? O YES O NO

4. Are you able to be 100% transparent and honest with someone you're dating or in a relationship with? O YES O NO

Are You Distrusting? (check any that apply to you)

1. Is it hard for you to trust others? O YES O NO

2. Do you often feel like you have to look over your shoulder? O YES O NO

3. Do you find it hard to trust what people say or do, even though they never gave you a clear reason to distrust them? O YES O NO

4. Have you ever found yourself obsessing over what a significant other is doing when they're not with you? O YES O NO

5. Do you feel the need to check your significant other's phone, texts, social media, or email? O YES O NO

6. Have you ever justified being controlling as a result of distrust? O YES O NO

Are You Controlling? (check any that apply to you)

1. Is it difficult to admit when you're wrong? O YES O NO

2. Does it bother you when people don't do or see things your way? O YES O NO

3. Do you take on too much because you don't trust things will get done right? O YES O NO

4. Have you ever decided to do something yourself because the person helping you wasn't doing things your way? O YES O NO

5. Do ever experience anxiety at the thought that something may not go the way you want or desire? O YES O NO

6. If yes to #5, does that anxiety ever lead you to do things you ordinarily wouldn't so that you can get the outcome you desire? O YES O NO

Toxic Tendencies Worksheet

Are You Possessive? (check any that apply to you)

1. Do you forsake all others when you enter a new relationship? ◯ YES ◯ NO

2. Has your idea of "loving hard" ever been described as clingy? ◯ YES ◯ NO

3. Do you have a tendency to cut yourself off from family/friends in a relationship and expect your significant other to do the same? ◯ YES ◯ NO

4. Have you ever found it so difficult to be away from a significant other that you've jeopardized your job or other relationships to be with them? ◯ YES ◯ NO

5. Have you ever been described as possessive in any of your other relationships (children, parents, friends, siblings, romantic)? ◯ YES ◯ NO

Do You Have a Savior Complex? (check any that apply to you)

1. Do you believe that you can "love" someone into being who you need them to be? ◯ YES ◯ NO

2. Have you spent more time hoping someone toxic would change rather than seeing their inability or unwillingness to change? ◯ YES ◯ NO

3. Have you ever known that you needed to walk away from a relationship but felt like you were abandoning them? ◯ YES ◯ NO

4. Have you felt accountable or responsible for someone you loved, even though they were toxic? ◯ YES ◯ NO

5. Have you ever gone out of your way to diagnose someone's behavior in order to justify not "abandoning" them? ◯ YES ◯ NO

Are You The Victim in Most Situations? (check any that apply to you)

1. Is it hard for you to empathize or see another person's perspective? ◯ YES ◯ NO

2. In an argument or disagreement, do you spend more time expressing how you feel without trying to understand where the other person is coming from? ◯ YES ◯ NO

3. Do you avoid accepting criticism by becoming defensive, shifting criticism back to the other person, or avoiding accountability? ◯ YES ◯ NO

4. Do you find it difficult to apologize when you're wrong? ◯ YES ◯ NO

5. Is it difficult for you to hear your faults, or self-reflect on how you could be/do better? ◯ YES ◯ NO

Toxic Tendencies Worksheet

Are You Attention-Seeking? (check any that apply to you)

1. Do you demand constant attention from your significant other in a relationship? ⬤ YES ⬤ NO

2. If your significant other doesn't pay you enough attention, do you turn to social media or people of the opposite sex to validate you? ⬤ YES ⬤ NO

3. If you posted something on social media that didn't get a lot of "likes" or engagement, do you become angry or disappointed? ⬤ YES ⬤ NO

4. Do you use sex or your sex appeal to get or keep your significant other's attention? ⬤ YES ⬤ NO

5. If your significant other doesn't pay you enough attention, are you quick to suspect that something is wrong in the relationship? ⬤ YES ⬤ NO

Are You Insecure? (check any that apply to you)

1. Do you "lead" with what you can give in new relationships (i.e. sex, money, gifts, etc.), as a way to purchase their loyalty early on? ⬤ YES ⬤ NO

2. Are you hyper-critical or do you have a habit of constantly pointing out your significant other's flaws? ⬤ YES ⬤ NO

3. Are you overly-critical of yourself and worry that you'll never be enough for your significant other? ⬤ YES ⬤ NO

4. Do you avoid disagreements (major or minor) because you're afraid of jeopardizing your relationship? ⬤ YES ⬤ NO

5. Do you find yourself feeling like you have to "work" for your partner's love in relationships out of fear of losing them? ⬤ YES ⬤ NO

6. Are you terrified of being abandoned in relationships, often creating an unhealthy level of dependency on those you love? ⬤ YES ⬤ NO

Take Moment to Reflect ———————————————

Thank you for taking the time to thoroughly complete the Toxic Tendencies section. This was an empowerment tool. When you are willing to admit your own tendencies, you can be more sensitive to these behaviors and recognize them when they emerge. Your emotions and your thoughts are directly related to your behavior. When you are in tune with yourself, you will begin to recognize when your emotions and thoughts are provoking behavior. The goal is to be able to course-correct before acting on impulse.

This level of honesty is not easy to submit to, so it's okay if it took you a few days to complete. It's important for you to see that this exercise was not about beating yourself up or forcing you to take blame for the failure of your relationships. It was about opening your eyes and being honest with yourself about flaws that perhaps facilitated environments that nurtured toxicity. Now that you've taken an honest look in the mirror, you can identify the person you no longer wish to be.

In this next writing exercise, we want you to take a moment to think about any of your toxic tendencies that may have been revealed to you. This exercise came after you "named" your enemies because we wanted you to be able to see the direct correlation between your past relationships and any behaviors that you have adapted, whether for coping or self-preservation. Before you continue, go review the places where you named your enemies. Do you see the inception of any of your toxic tendencies?

Now that you've had a chance to complete the "Toxic Tendencies" worksheet, were there any toxic tendencies that you didn't realize you had? Where do you these "tendencies" come from? (hint: revisit the areas where you named your enemies, you could have been conditioned by those relationships).

Which toxic tendencies did you notice *within you* that possibly facilitated the environment that made your ex or other toxic people comfortable in being toxic *towards you*? How so?

Facing Your Final Enemy ——————————————

———————————————— ♌ ————————————————

"The thief comes only to steal and kill and destroy; I have come that they may have life, and have it to the full." **John 10:10 (NIV)**

Finally, there is one more enemy that needs to be recognized. While your heartbreak and subsequent pain are extremely important right now, we want to call to your attention all of the other relationships that have been impacted by everything you're experiencing: your family, your friends, yourself, maybe your children, and, most importantly, God. Understand that the enemy desires to disconnect and distract you from everything that has the power to uplift you right now, and that especially includes Christ.

Remember when we stated that God is relationship personified? God is also life personified. To keep you from God is to keep you from life and keep you in death. This enemy will use whatever and whoever it takes to overwhelm you with things you might feel are more important than your relationship with God. He'll use good relationships, negative relationships, personal pleasure, prosperity, success, and even paralyzing hurt. Whatever gets your attention, the enemy will use it in an attempt to destroy you and condemn you to death.

Let's look at some scripture:

"For our struggle is not against flesh and blood, but against the rulers, against the authorities, against the powers of this dark world and against the spiritual forces of evil in the heavenly realms." Ephesians 6:12 NIV

- While you struggle with the pain of your circumstance, the enemy hopes to use that circumstance to hinder, stop, or derail your relationship with God.

"Be alert and of sober mind. Your enemy the devil prowls around like a roaring lion looking for someone to devour." 1 Peter 5:8 NIV

- Even now, be alert and aware of how this circumstance has caused you to feel, think, and behave.

- Going through this doesn't mean that God has forsaken you. It means God has been with you because it didn't destroy you.

"If you do what is right, will you not be accepted? But if you do not do what is right, sin is crouching at your door; it desires to have you, but you must rule over it." Genesis 4:7 NIV

- Your anger, hurt, resentment, vindictiveness, desires, and habits are all waiting for you to respond. But you got this. You can rule over this mood and this moment.

"The one who does what is sinful is of the devil, because the devil has been sinning from the beginning. The reason the Son of God appeared was to destroy the devil's work." 1 John 3:8 NIV

- The devil's work is to separate you from God.
- Christ is your answer to that work. The way you fight back is through Christ.

"Since the children have flesh and blood, he too shared in their humanity so that by his death he might break the power of him who holds the power of death—that is, the devil." Hebrews 2:14 NIV

- Christ is your answer because He understands you.
- Christ is your answer because He knows you.
- Christ is here with you in this moment so that, even in this process, your relationship with God will not suffer.

"Submit yourselves, then, to God. Resist the devil, and he will flee from you." James 4:7 NIV

- If Christ is your answer, this is how you answer with Christ.
- Submit to God, not just your life, but also your concerns, even this soul-tie.
- You resist the devil when you submit to God.

"Do not be anxious about anything, but in every situation, by prayer and petition, with thanksgiving, present your requests to God. And the peace of God, which transcends all understanding, will guard your hearts and your minds in Christ Jesus." Philippians 4:6-7 NIV

- The devil is your enemy.
- Give your concerns and yourself to God.
- Christ is your answer.

YOU GOT THIS!

"

Going through this doesn't
mean that God has forsaken
you. It means God has been
with you...because it didn't
destroy you.

Facing the Final Enemy Exercise

Complete the following prayer:

Father God, I come to you through Jesus the Christ, my mediator and savior. I come to you to tell you that I am (*Write out how you feel, and be honest. Example: I am hurt. I am disappointed. I am tired.*)

_____

_____

_____

_____

(*Write out the name of all enemies, not including yourself*)

_____

_____

_____

_____

I know I could have made better decisions too. I confess (*Write out your confession of decisions made that you know could have been better. Be totally honest.*)

_____

_____

_____

_____

_____

_____

_____

_____

But as of right now, I've decided to choose you.

Please receive me, even from this broken place. I know that you have the power to restore me to better than I have ever been.

Please forgive me.
I don't want to be who I was.
I want to be who you would have me to be.
I want to be used by you.
Help me be a better instrument of your will.

As I give my heart to you, Father, please receive the burdens of my heart. They are much too heavy for me. Place your hand on my pain and begin to heal it. As you heal my pain, direct me, guide me, and counsel me through your Holy Spirit.

Protect me, Father, from (*Write the names of all your enemies.*)

_____

_____

_____

_____

Protect me, Father, from Satan and spiritual wickedness. Protect me, Father, from what I don't see or can't identify as a danger to me, my well-being, or my relationship with you. (*Add anything to this prayer that is on your heart at this time*)

_____

_____

_____

_____

_____

_____

Thank you for being my help.

Thank you for your consistent presence and love.

In the name of Christ I pray these things,

Amen.

Remember this always:

"The steadfast love of the Lord never ceases; his mercies never come to an end; they are new every morning; great is your faithfulness."
Lamentations 3:22-23 NIV

66

While you struggle with the
pain of your circumstance,
the enemy hopes to use that
circumstance to hinder, stop,
or derail your relationship
with God...But GOD!

Capture Every Thought

_ℓℓ_

"The weapons we fight with are not the weapons of the world. On the contrary, they have divine power to demolish strongholds. We demolish arguments and every pretension that sets itself up against the knowledge of God, and we take captive every thought to make it obedient to Christ." **2 Corinthians 10:4-5 (NIV)**

In 2 Corinthians 10, Paul is explaining how he wages a divine war that breaks the strongholds of bad reasoning, as well as destroys false arguments. His weapon of choice is what he describes as "capturing every thought" and bringing them under subjection to God. The principle in Paul's letter is not just applicable for the kingdom, it's also applicable for how you can manage yourself and your emotions while you're healing.

You can't alleviate or avoid your feelings. You can't stop certain thoughts from entering your mind. And even when you're healed and moving forward, you will still think about things that have the ability to flood you with all kinds of emotions. Healing doesn't mean you won't think certain thoughts; healing means you can handle whatever thought comes into your mind. You start handling your thoughts by capturing them and making your thoughts serve you.

How to Capture Your Thoughts ——————

Your feelings are valid responses to what you believe is happening to you. They are naturally responsive to your thoughts and become the catalyst for your actions. Everything you do (good or bad) from the moment you take action is a direct result of your thoughts and how you allowed them to make you feel. The goal is to be able to stop and recognize what thoughts will trigger certain responses from you and reframe those thoughts while also being able to identify when you're being overwhelmed by your feelings.

Since feelings are responsive, we want to take them out of the driver's seat whenever possible. We aren't going to give you instructions on how to deny your feelings. We're going to show you how to reframe and repurpose any thoughts that do not serve you before they mature into behavior. Remember your head, your heart, and your hand switches? This exercise will help you continue to manage them appropriately.

This will be another written exercise for your journal. It's important to actually practice taking a "time out" to write, especially when you're emotionally overwhelmed. These moments put you back in control, which is ultimately what you want. Use the below questions to lead you through that process.

Whenever you recognize a negative thought imposing unwanted feelings: ————

1. Acknowledge your thoughts: What is the thought that just entered your mind? Then answer the following questions about what you're thinking in that moment.

    a. What's going on in your surroundings that brought this up?

    b. Is this thought based on facts, fear, or assumptions (and where is it coming from)?

    c. Is this thought healthy for you and your environment?

    d. What usually happens if you allow yourself to continue to follow these thoughts?

Now, acknowledge what you're feeling in that moment, then reframe your thoughts so it is more realistic and healthier for you.

Example:

What is the thought(s) that just entered your mind?

"I'm never going to have the kind of love I deserve!"

    a. **What's going on in your surroundings that brought this up?** *Watching Grey's Anatomy. I love Derek and Meredith's love.*

    b. **Is this thought based on facts, fear, or assumptions?** *Fear. Because I keep getting my heart broken, I'm afraid I'm going to keep ending up hurt and alone.*

c. Is this thought healthy for you and your environment? *Definitely not.*

d. What usually happens if you allow yourself to continue to follow these thoughts? *I'll emotionally spiral out of control. I'll probably end up calling them or taking them back because, out of fear and loneliness, I'll convince myself that having them is better than no one at all.*

2. Give yourself permission and the space to feel whatever it is that you feel.

a. Whenever your thoughts begin to overwhelm you, use the formula in step one to either talk yourself through it or write them out. Hiding from your feelings only relocates them to another place that will force you to face them again later. Acknowledging them and understanding them puts them in their proper place.

b. After processing your feelings, finish this sentence:

I know I feel like this right now, but I'm going to be okay because

_____

3. Acknowledge the harmful actions being provoked by how you feel.

a. Whenever you feel like this, what does it make you want to do?

b. By stating what your feelings are driving you to do, you can now answer these questions regarding your actions:

i. Is what you feel like doing healthy for you and your environment?

ii. How will doing what you feel like doing hinder your progress?

iii. What happened the last time you did this or something similar? How did you end up feeling afterwards?

iv. What is something that you can do to redirect your attention and energy (so your feelings don't mature into harmful actions)?

Continue to pray about your thoughts and feelings and be intentional about capturing them. Always remember that you don't have to face everything when it comes to you. So if a situation arises, and it is not pressing or urgent, remove yourself from it. Work through the "Capturing Your Thoughts" exercise and then take no less than 20 minutes to redirect your energy.

Take a picture of this exercise and save it in your phone so you can quickly access it when you need it.

Facing the Enemy Closing Assignment

By now, your journal has been filled with emotionally stirring accounts of pain. You can look back and see that you have identified and denounced your enemies, as you clean up your emotional and spiritual environment. There are just two more things to do this week.

Read – Go back to the beginning of your assignments this week and read (out loud) everything that you have written. This is an important part of the process. When you read your truths and your prayers out loud, you are committing them to memory. This process literally positions you to accept and move on from the things you cannot change, empowers you to change the things you can, and gives you insight on the difference. So read.

Pray – Continue to write out your prayers daily. One day, you will be able to look back and see how God has answered your prayers.

Phase Four Small Group Discussion Questions

1. Who or what was the greatest enemy you had to face during this phase?
2. Why do you think it is so important to face the people who have hurt us and label them as an enemy?
3. What helped you get through this part of the process?

Phase four is a two-week process. If you have not used up your full two-weeks, use this next week to review and complete the journal assignment as thoroughly as possible. Then, rest.

PHASE FIVE

FORGIVENESS

"Get rid of all bitterness, rage and anger, brawling and slander, along with every form of malice. Be kind and compassionate to one another, forgiving each other, just as in Christ God forgave you." **Ephesians 4:31-32 (NIV)**

Phase Five: Forgiveness

Welcome to forgiveness week. At this point, you have spent two weeks taking inventory of your enemies, so you should no longer be in denial about who and what they are. You've faced the past enemies of your youth and the more recent enemies of your adulthood. You've faced some personal accountabilities as well. Now that you've faced some difficult truths from your past, you have the awareness and the authority to take control of your future.

This week you will take every corpse that you spent the last two weeks digging up and bury them. No shallow graves here. You will need to dig extra deep. You're going to lay these enemies to rest, and the dirt that you will pour over their graves is forgiveness.

What Is Forgiveness

Remember the saying, "Refusing to forgive someone is like drinking poison and waiting for the other person to die"? It sounds like all we have to do is to forgive them so that we can feel better. That's not true. It is unfortunate, but many of us have been force-fed a false idea of forgiveness. We have been taught that forgiveness means that we are emotionally well, personally healed, and have gotten over what was done to us. We're taught to put on a smile and act as if nothing ever happened and to ignore the pain that people have caused.

And we're supposed to do it effortlessly while we're at it. It's sad, but we have been led to believe that forgiving people this way is actually the best thing for us. The truth is that not drinking the poison, doesn't mean you're going to feel better, it just means you survived.

Struggling to "forgive and forget" can cause you more harm than the actual pain of the brokenness itself. Because this is the version of forgiveness that has been perpetuated. Because of that perspective, allowing yourself to feel the pain of your past, and even responding to it, seems like a betrayal to the forgiveness process. You begin to gaslight yourself into believing that because you still feel pain, your forgiveness is invalid. You may even question your Christianity or godliness. Carrying on this way will cause you to avoid forgiveness because, based on this ideology, the pain only reinforces how messed up you are. This is self-denigrating agony.

The truth is, forgiveness doesn't make you happy. It doesn't change your mood nor is it an indication that something has changed. Forgiveness doesn't make you more hospitable or friendly to the enemy. It certainly doesn't mean that you are over whatever caused you pain. And you are not required to forget. The reality of forgiveness is that you still may have emotional pain that you have to deal with for a long period of time.

Forgiveness is releasing someone from a debt that they owe you. While this would seem like forgiveness alleviates consequences, it doesn't. It simply removes the burden of making sure they suffer those consequences from you. You can't move on from people if you remain present just to administer consequences. That keeps you in some form of a relationship with them. You essentially become an emotional bill collector who is following up to make sure they pay.

There is a reason why companies outsource their collections. It costs those companies more than the debt owed by the customers to chase the customers and force payment. It's less expensive for companies to write off the debt (forgive) so that they can move forward without any attachment to the delinquent party. Forgiveness means no more relationship with the customer, so the company can move on.

You cannot afford to spend your life chasing what you believe you are owed. The chase will keep you perpetually connected to them and you'll pay a price that is far too emotionally and mentally expensive. Forgive and then give it to your professional debt collector: God.

We understand how difficult it is to hand things over to God because it seems like He will simply forgive and forget as well. Yet, when you read Deuteronomy 32:35 (NIV), God says, "It is mine to avenge; I will repay. In due time their foot will slip; their day of disaster is near and their doom rushes upon them." This entire passage is full of consequence. God states that He wants to seek vengeance on your behalf. He knew this burden would be too heavy for you. Release it to Him. Their consequences are no longer your concern.

Do I Forget?

We would strongly advise against forgetting the harm done to you. The idea of forgetting is a metaphor meaning you wouldn't continue to punish or remind people of the hurt they've caused you. But when people show you their capacity to mistreat you or take advantage of you, they've set a precedent for who they are. You don't forget this, you learn from it. Committing their behavior to memory empowers you to make the necessary choices to protect yourself from them later.

Let's say you own a store and you've hired a cashier to manage the register. However, when you balance your ledger, you find out that this trusted clerk has been consistently stealing from the cash register. Now you're out of the money, you need to restock supplies, you have one less trusted employee, and you're personally upset because you handpicked and chose them yourself. However, you still decide to forgive them of the debt.

Even though you forgave:

- Are you still missing the money?
- Do you still need to pay your bills?
- As thieves, are they safe for your business?
- As thieves, would you still consider them employable?
- Are you required to forget what they stole and act as if it never happened?

Forgiveness doesn't erase the debt, it doesn't eliminate your bills, and it certainly doesn't change who they are. Forgiveness changes the context of your relationship with them and eliminates what they owe to you. That's it.

When people hurt you, swallowing your pain or sweeping it under the rug will not serve you. Acknowledging how it made you feel and assigning responsibility for your hurt is essential. Whether or not you confront them about it or terminate the relationship is up to you. Whether or not they accept responsibility is not your problem. Your primary goal is to handle your hurt in a healthy way so that you can properly carry out the process of forgiveness.

Forgiveness does not:

- Re-establish trust.
- Heal the pain of loss.
- Free them from consequence.
- Mean they are guiltless.
- Mean reconciliation.
- Re-establish access to you.

Maintaining Your Peace in the Midst of Forgiveness

Even in the face of forgiveness, it's important to make sure that your environment is safe as you heal. The journey to forgiveness and peace will not be smooth. You'll be reminded of things that disturb your mood, and some days you will have to push forward when you don't feel like it. Some of you will even have children whose environments you need to keep safe as well. This is where you will have to practice the tools provided to you such as the head, hands, and heart visualizations, capturing your thoughts, and reading those affirmations that we introduced you to. Maintaining your peace requires you to maintain awareness of the things (or thoughts) that can disrupt your environment and put in intentional effort to reject or reframe those thoughts or situations.

Triggers

Triggers are neurological and emotional responses to either mentally reliving our traumas or the fears we have of reliving our traumas. Traumatic experiences like being betrayed, abused, or rejected create opportunities for these triggers. Even though it can sometimes seem as if an event no longer affects us, triggers tend to embed themselves in our conscious and subconscious minds and remind us of what we are afraid of when we least expect it.

Forgiveness won't stop triggers, and just because you still experience triggers doesn't mean that you haven't forgiven them. You will still have emotional responses to things that feel familiar. Healing from them doesn't happen at forgiveness, it happens as you move forward.

Happiness

Happiness is not a place you arrive at after forgiveness. Forgiveness allows you to let go so that you can move forward on your way to happiness. So it's important to not try to force yourself to appear or be happy. Of course we want you to be able to gradually move towards a place of inner peace and happiness, but you can't occupy that place without first allowing yourself this time to grieve. You don't have to fake happiness to affirm that you forgave them. You don't have to fake a smile as proof either. You're going to be sad despite your forgiveness, and that is a part of your healing journey. Happiness will come. Keep moving forward.

Anger

Even after you've forgiven someone, anger may still come and go. Forgiveness doesn't get rid of the anger, it just alters your response to it. Before, anger used to destroy your day or make you want to give them a piece of your mind. Now, forgiveness will enable you to pause and remember that God is your avenger. Release your anger to God at every turn. He's never lost a battle.

Peace ────────────────────

Peace doesn't imply happiness, nor does it imply painlessness. Peace is a place of relief and rest. It's the relief of not being weighed down by a war with the enemy. No more anxiety, no more stress, no more heartache. When you make the decision to forgive, peace begins to form. When the weight of vengeance is lifted by giving it to God, you can be at rest.

Will you still be angry? Sure, but you won't allow yourself to stay there. Will you still be triggered? Yes, but you have the tools to remind yourself of your reality. Will you have many different emotions? Yes, but even in those emotions, you'll be able to soothe yourself to a place of peace. Forgiveness reminds you to direct your energy and concern to yourself so you are not preoccupied with them. Be at peace.

Be the Consequence ─────────────

We get it. Giving your anger and hurt to God, and not seeking vengeance for the people who hurt you, is so anticlimactic, especially after everything you've given and been through! At the very least, you want closure. While it does not feel like they are getting what they deserve, you have to trust that losing you and losing control over you is the best consequence.

Forgiving them, moving on, and living a life unbothered by them is the consequence. Allowing yourself to healthily grieve them and heal from them is their consequence. All of this allows you to move on without them, and that's the greatest consequence of all.

Self-Forgiveness: The Grace of Personal Release

After walking so many people through this program, we noticed how important it was to address this topic. Many have come to us heavily burdened with guilt and shame. That guilt and shame tended to multiply as they personally accounted for things that they could've done differently in past relationships. To help people release that inward guilt and shame, in the past we worked on self-forgiveness. But as believers, it's important to understand that self-forgiveness is not necessary.

We understand the need for personal absolution. We understand the desire to create a line in the sand that clearly identifies the place where you made a decision to be different. Tradition has taught us that there has to be an act of unloading personal mistakes and moving forward. That's all ok, unload it, but that's not self-forgiveness. That's walking in forgiveness.

Biblically, there is no precedent for self-forgiveness, and there's a good reason for that. We cannot save ourselves. Remember what we said in the beginning of this book? God seeks our participation in His rescue.

God is the only one who has the power (or the need) to forgive you. Your participation is accepting it.

"I, even I, am he who blots out your transgressions, for my own sake, and remembers your sins no more." Isaiah 43:25 NIV

"Why does this fellow talk like that? He's blaspheming! Who can forgive sins but God alone?" Mark 2:7 NIV

God's nature requires forgiveness for those He loves.

When God forgives:

- It's a statement that you have sinned.
- It's a statement that He loves you despite that sin.
- It's a statement that He has determined that you are not defined by your sin.
- It's a statement that you are clear and free and cannot be personally connected to whatever you did.

If God forgives you, then your mistakes are removed and "blotted out" by someone greater than you. Receive that!

People tend to hang on to what they've done out of a toxic shame. It's hard to stop replaying the entire situation when you keep telling yourself that you should have known better. It's hard to let go of the shame when you saw who they were, but you stayed in the relationship anyway. Toxic shame is a learned response that causes you to repeatedly punish yourself for an internally perceived flaw. It lies to you by making you feel like you are your mistake. Toxic shame holds you back. And as long as it is allowed to torment you, you will continue to beat yourself and cast yourself into your own hell. But it doesn't have to be this way.

Read: John 8:1-11 NIV

1 But Jesus went to the Mount of Olives.

2 At dawn he appeared again in the temple courts, where all the people gathered around him, and he sat down to teach them. 3 The teachers of the law and the Pharisees brought in a woman caught in adultery. They made her stand before the group 4 and said to Jesus, "Teacher, this woman was caught in the act of adultery. 5 In the Law Moses commanded us to stone such women. Now what do you say?" 6 They were using this question as a trap, in order to have a basis for accusing him.

But Jesus bent down and started to write on the ground with his finger. 7 When they kept on questioning him, he straightened up and said to them, "Let any one of you who is without sin be the first to throw a stone at her." 8 Again he stooped down and wrote on the ground.

9 At this, those who heard began to go away one at a time, the older ones first, until only Jesus was left, with the woman still standing there. 10 Jesus straightened up and asked her, "Woman, where are they? Has no one condemned you?"

11 "No one, sir," she said.

"Then neither do I condemn you," Jesus declared. "Go now and leave your life of sin."

One of the first things we see in this passage is the fact that this woman was guilty and Jesus did not ignore her guilt. He confronted it. There was no question regarding what was done, and everyone knew the consequences. The only concern Jesus had was what to do about what was done. Jesus addressed all the guilty people present. They were fully ready to stone her. But if she was guilty enough to be stoned to death, then they were too.

After setting them straight, Jesus focused upon addressing her guilt. He first asked if there is anyone there to condemn her. Her guilt required condemnation, there just wasn't anyone who had the true power to condemn her. The crowd couldn't condemn her, and more importantly, nor could she. Christ, being the only one having the authority to judge, told her she was not condemned by Him. He knew what she did and forgave her. Then Jesus gave her instructions after forgiveness. He told her to go and not do it anymore. There was no additional step of self-forgiveness. She received Christ's absolution and then walked in it.

You do not need to forgive yourself, because you are forgiven. You may carry the emotional baggage of shame, but to God you are no longer guilty. All God asks is that you do not do anything else that will put you in this same place again. Obedience should be your only response, not self-punishment.

Go and sin no more.

Releasing Yourself ─────────────

Releasing yourself is acknowledging that you're forgiven. Receiving Christ's forgiveness breaks your bondage. As a result, you disconnect from your past. You give yourself permission to move ahead. You break another part of that soul-tie.

Where Are Those Who Condemn You? ─────────

We all have felt the emotional punishment of shame. When others try to punish us with shame, they want us to be perpetually humiliated and define us by what we've done. They want us to feel unworthy, unloved, and of no value. That's when toxic shame becomes abusive. Toxic shame is how people who have hurt you got you to accept their behavior. It's what they will attempt to use to bully themselves back into your life.

Jesus Christ asks you right now, "Where are those who condemn you?"

- They don't have the right to condemn or shame you.
- You don't have the right to condemn or shame you.
- Through Jesus, you are not condemned nor shamed.

The Process of Release ——————————

For the release that you need, you will first need to receive forgiveness from the highest authority: Christ. Identify what you are guilty of and what causes you to feel shame. Then receive that Christ has already paid the consequence for you. Receive His payment and be renewed.

Notes
—————————— ℓℓ ——————————

Eight Affirmations for Releasing Shame

1. I am loved and I am forgiven.
2. There is nothing that I can do that will stop God from loving me.
3. Because I am forgiven, I am released from the debt of my mistakes.
4. My mistakes are a part of my story, but they do not define me.
5. Choosing to move forward doesn't betray my truth, it honors God's forgiveness.
6. I am wholly deserving of every good thing coming to me. Nothing in my past can stop me from receiving good things.
7. Because I am in Christ, no one has the right to condemn me to shame.
8. I will defeat shame daily by sharing my testimony of wholeness and forgiveness.

In order for affirmations to have a believable impact in your life, it's important to practice saying them out loud whenever you feel the burden of shame coming on you. We'd even recommend recording yourself reciting these on your phone so that you can hear your voice releasing yourself from shame.

Forgiveness Exercise

In this week's journal entries, you will write your declarations of forgiveness to those who have hurt you. Use the entries from Facing the Enemy to be specific.

Write the following sentence for each person that you need to forgive:

"I forgive [insert name]. I release them from any debt to me and entrust them to God's justice. [Name], you are released."

After you've completed writing down all the people that you've released to God, read it all out loud to yourself. Reading aloud is a statement of declaration.

Disclaimer:

There is no need to read your declarations of forgiveness to the individuals on your list. You don't even have to tell them that you forgive them. They have no power to keep you from forgiving them. This is all between you and God.

Declarations of Forgiveness

_____
(Their Name)

I release them from any debt to me and entrust them to God's justice.

_____ You are released.
(Their Name)

_____
(Their Name)

I release them from any debt to me and entrust them to God's justice.

_____ You are released.

_____
(Their Name)

I release them from any debt to me and entrust them to God's justice.

_____ You are released.

_____
(Their Name)

I release them from any debt to me and entrust them to God's justice.

_____ You are released.

_____
(Their Name)

I release them from any debt to me and entrust them to God's justice.

_____ You are released.

_____
(Their Name)

I release them from any debt to me and entrust them to God's justice.

_____ You are released.

_____
(Their Name)

I release them from any debt to me and entrust them to God's justice.

_____ You are released.

_____
(Their Name)

I release them from any debt to me and entrust them to God's justice.

_____ You are released.

_____
(Their Name)

I release them from any debt to me and entrust them to God's justice.

_____ You are released.

_____
(Their Name)

I release them from any debt to me and entrust them to God's justice.

_____ You are released.

_____
(Their Name)

I release them from any debt to me and entrust them to God's justice.

_____ You are released.

A Prayer of Release

Father God, these are those who have done me harm. They've caused me to grieve and caused me to question myself and you. I was bound to them, and while I know these ties are being broken, I am still affected by them.

Today, Father, I release them into your justice. Father God, I trust your wisdom and will for their lives. I trust that you are my healer, provider, caretaker, and avenger. You are my Abba Father.

Please continue your healing work within me. Let me be more sensitive towards the presence, direction, and counsel of your Holy Spirit.

Thank you so much for your everlasting love and kindness. Amen.

A Prayer of Self-Release

Father God, thank you for being willing to forgive me. I have done things that I knew were not right or good. And while I know you have forgiven me, I continue to walk in shame.

Please, Father, let your Holy Spirit search my heart for any residue of the past and clean it. Please forgive my mistakes, my choices, and my thoughts that did not and do not reflect you. Search me, oh Lord, and clean me through Christ. Make me new.

Today I receive your forgiveness and I am released. Because you are the authority over my life, I trust my life in your care. Because your mercy is sufficient, I receive it for myself.

Thank you for your forgiveness. Heal me, strengthen me, guide me, and quicken me to live the life you have for me.

Because God has forgiven me, I am released from condemnation. Because God has released me, I let go of my guilt, shame, and self-condemnation.

We, Kenyon and Taccara, both stand in agreement with you, in the Name of Jesus the Christ. Continue to journal daily prayers.

Phase Five Small Group Discussion Questions

1. How would you explain forgiveness in light of what you learned?
2. This chapter dispels the idea behind forgiving and forgetting. How did it make you feel to learn that it was okay to forgive while continuing to remember what someone does to hurt you?
3. Even though the book proved that it is unnecessary to forgive yourself, why do people still struggle with the idea of self-forgiveness?
4. How do you feel about the affirmations for releasing shame? Will you continue to use them for yourself?

This is the end of Week Five. Please take time to review your prayers and complete your exercises.

"

Receiving Christ's forgiveness breaks your bondage. As a result, you disconnect from your past.

WEEK SIX

PHASE SIX

FREEDOM FORWARD

"Out of my deep anguish and pain I prayed, and God, you helped me as a father. You came to my rescue and broke open the way into a beautiful and broad place. Now I know, Lord, that you are for me, and I will never fear what man can do to me. For you stand beside me as my hero who rescues me. I've seen with my own eyes the defeat of my enemies. I've triumphed over them all!" **PS 118:5-7 (TPT)**

Phase Six: Freedom Forward

This is your last week with us. This week represents a graduation of your consistent efforts to break toxic bonds. You have come a long way. You've been focused, and even if you've fallen, you got up and kept pushing. You've been vigilant in protecting your physical, mental, and emotional environments. You've gotten through something you never thought you'd get through. You didn't just survive, you won.

You are effectively graduating from heartbreak to wholeness. However, graduation is not a stopping point; it's a commencement, a new beginning. When you first began this process, you were distraught and disoriented from the hurt you were experiencing. Now that you have begun taking back control of your life, it's easy to believe that everything is miraculously okay and that you should return back to the way things were. You've made a lot of changes to your heart, your mind, and your environment. If you want to maintain your freedom, nothing can go back to the way things were.

In your new-found freedom, we want to caution you against becoming complacent or letting your guard down. Everyone should not be welcomed into your promised land. There will still be environments that are unsafe for your continued growth. Freedom from them does not mean you are done *becoming*. Freedom means that you have changed your mind about who you've been. As you are being molded into someone new, you will soon recognize that there will be people and places that you will no longer fit in with.

Beware of Pitfalls Ahead

In times of stress or sadness, human nature will always tempt us to revert back to our comfort zones. From triggers to toxic relationships, our habits have become a comfort zone for us. Going back to those things, even if they're not good for us, can feel safe. As good and confident as you may feel, everything can shift in an instant. You will be tested, people from your past will try to re-enter your life, and you will be triggered and flooded with emotions at times. This is where you will have to make the choice to either go back to what feels safe or fight for your new normal. Remaining aware of how various surroundings can impact you gives you the ability to "course correct" before your habits take over.

From Slaves to Citizens

We continue to use Exodus as our blueprint for deliverance because the narrative has principles of deliverance embedded in the story. Your journey is only beginning, so these principles will carry you through the next phase.

The people of Israel were oppressed by the Egyptians both physically and mentally. As slaves, they formed a relationship with the Egyptian culture. Egyptian customs, false idols, and wealth had become a part of who the Israelites were. Even though they were slaves, they became comfortable in the discomfort of captivity, so much so that after Israel escaped and times got difficult, many wanted to go back to what they were accustomed to in Egypt. Suddenly, what was once considered a toxic relationship wasn't that bad anymore. Delivering them from Egypt physically was only the start of the work. God had to deliver the mentalities that they had become accustomed to as well. Otherwise, the Israelites would revert back to who they were as slaves.

God delivered Israel in stages or phases. The first phase of this blueprint was the emotional deliverance. They had to emotionally experience discomfort in their environment to help them understand why it was no longer safe. When people become comfortable in toxicity, sometimes it's hard for them to truly grasp the impact of it. No matter how bad it seems, toxicity is able to kill slowly because it is often mixed with comfort that helps camouflage the effects. God had to help them come to terms with how badly they were really being treated before they would ever be convinced to leave.

First, God had to build their confidence in Him. Since they were in captivity for so long, they didn't know if God would help. God had to give them the personal confidence to follow His lead out of that relationship.

Knowing God was with you wasn't permission to stay in a bad place, it was a signal to prepare to leave.

Then God showed Israel that He was willing to deliver them out of that situation. God showed them that He was adamant about rescuing them. When God stretched out his hand for them to come out of bondage, it gave them the courage to reach back in obedience.

God's will for you is that you be rescued. But in order to be rescued, you have to participate by reaching back out to Him.

Finally, while demonstrating His power to His people, God proceeded to frustrate the oppressor. Egypt fell under a curse, and every plague made Israel a liability to have around. Pharaoh hated them, but his pride made him determined to keep control over them. Frustrating the oppressor ensured that Israel had to leave. It made the environment so bad that they were no longer safe. It would never be the same again. Israel had become the bane of Egypt's existence. There was no turning back.

Perhaps you had an incident that broke the relationship irreparably. It was the last straw where you knew things would never be the same again. That should be the point where there was no going back. No fixing things or trying to put things back together. You had to go.

The decision to leave wasn't easy and it wasn't comfortable for the Israelites. God's presence is what sheltered them, guided them, and instructed them. That same presence has also been with you.

The second phase of this blueprint was God's physical deliverance. Israel committed to their escape by being obedient to the plan God had laid out for them. When the time came, they left without hesitation.

Perhaps you can relate. Their oppressor told them to get out.

Then, as they walked out, they were aggressively pursued as if they were desired again. But they didn't look back, they kept going forward. They were scared to death of what was behind them but also scared of what was ahead of them. Physically leaving was so hard because it left them in the midst of so much uncertainty. So naturally, they were tempted to go back to what they knew.

The third phase of this blueprint was the mental deliverance. Israel left Egypt physically, but not mentally. So while God could have shown Israel a shortcut through Philistia to the promised land, He instead sent them the long way around. It wasn't a cruel joke. God knew that Israel was not mentally prepared to exist in the freedom they had been given. They had to be molded for their new reality, as a new nation. So God rerouted Israel through the wilderness. It is through this wilderness process that their paradigm was molded into a mentally free nation.

It was only when they were mentally and physically free that they were able to call themselves free. Being mentally free meant that they were no longer under the influence of their old habits and toxic relationships. They were able to identify and escape potentially dangerous situations and were beginning to trust their own voices again. They were a self-sufficient thriving nation under God. They were ready for the next phase.

The end of this book is not your promised land; that's ahead of you. The end of this book is a place that marks your mental evolution. You're different, so you must move differently to complete the trip. Perhaps some cravings, desires, habits, and thoughts are still dying off. That is par for the course. But the end of this book has positioned you to enter into a place of personal empowerment, peace, and wholeness.

It took Israel 40 years in the wilderness to undo over 400 years of trauma. We're not saying it will take you 40 years to be on the other side of this. We are saying it's going to take more than a month before you're ready to jump back into romantic relationships again. So, as tempting as it will be and as lonely as it may get, treat this next phase as your time alone to rediscover yourself after healing. In other words, don't jump into the next opportunity for intimacy that comes along. Relax into this new normal and new you.

Your Promised Land

> "The Lord gives strength to his people; the Lord blesses his people with peace."
> **Psalm 29:11 (NIV)**

The promised land was simply a place where Israel would be safe, secure, and at peace. God was responsible for providing for them, but they were accountable to God to keep it and maintain it. We want you to also be safe, secure, and at peace.

The promised land still had to be worked for. The children of Israel had to:

- Fight for the land.

- Set boundaries around them.

- Set up a system to protect their borders.

- Maintain their new, sterile environment.

- Re-introduce themselves to the world as a new nation.

Now that you have fought to break free from bondage, it will be important to continue what you learned in order to get you through this next period. You're going to have to fight against being placed in any kind of bondage again. You will need to establish healthy boundaries and standards for this next chapter. Then you'll re-introduce yourself to this world as a new and at-peace you.

Understanding Your Strengths and Weaknesses

There has been a lot of talk about the "new you," and we truly hope it is liberating to acknowledge the changes happening within you. You are in a season of empowerment and unlearning, and you are becoming a better, more focused version of yourself. However, in the process of unlearning certain behaviors and habits, it's important that you don't seek to unlearn the core of who you are.

It will be easy to try to get rid of your perceived weaknesses because you believe they are what made you a target for toxic people. From attempting to stop caring or "loving hard" to closing yourself off from letting people get close to you, or even when you blame yourself for attracting toxic people, these are all reasonable responses when you perceive yourself as weak. The truth is, falling in love with you is easy because you are strong, not because you are weak. Your weaknesses are merely your strengths being manipulated. We just need you to put your strengths and weaknesses in proper perspective so that you can identify how they can be manipulated or used against you.

In this next exercise, we are going to take a look at what makes you strong, both emotionally and mentally. Once you take inventory of those, we will help you see how they can be flipped to be used against you by a toxic person.

Strengths and Weaknesses

What Makes You Mentally Strong? (check any that apply to you)

○ I have very thick skin.

○ It takes a *lot* for me to get upset.

○ I'm an easy-going person.

○ Anything I put my mind to, I work hard to acheive it.

What Makes You Emotionally Strong? (check any that apply to you)

○ I can see the good in anyone.

○ I'm the "dependable" one in my circle.

○ It's easy for me to empathize with people.

○ It makes me happy to see those I love happy.

○ I love *hard* without discrimination.

○ I don't need a lot to be happy.

Now that you have taken inventory of your strengths, we're going to look at your strengths and show you how they translate into weaknesses under the right circumstances.

Strengths and Weaknesses

Your Strengths

O I have very thick skin.

O It takes a *lot* for me to get upset.

O I'm an easy-going person.

O Anything I put my mind to, I work hard to acheive it.

O I can see the good in anyone.

O I'm the "dependable" one in my circle.

O It's easy for me to empathize with people.

O It makes me happy to see those I love happy.

O I love *hard* without discrimination.

O I don't need a lot to be happy.

Strength Translated into Weakness

How this strength can become a weakness: It's easy for you to ignore or overlook when someone is mean or disrespectful towards you.

How this strength can become a weakness: You may avoid confronting situations when you are disrespected.

How this strength can become a weakness: You can be passive or shut down when people are blatantly toxic towards you.

How this strength can become a weakness: You will likely take on the responsibility of trying to change other people's bad behavior through your "good" behavior.

How this strength can become a weakness: You can ignore or overlook bad behavior.

How this strength can become a weakness: You can sometimes be guilted into enabling bad behavior.

How this strength can become a weakness: You treat people the way you would want to be treated, hoping they appreciate and reciprocate.

How this strength can become a weakness: You can be easily taken for granted because you genuinely want to see people happy.

How this strength can become a weakness: You love first and look later.

How this strength can become a weakness: It's easy for those you love to give you the bare minimum when you give them all of you.

This list was limited, but hopefully you get the picture. Can you think of any of your other strengths that have been manipulated and used against you in relationships? Write them down and try to identify how it enabled toxic behavior in past relationships.

Everything about who you are is amazing, and we will never encourage you to stop being what makes you uniquely you. The goal is to learn how to decipher who is deserving of all the benefits of you, and when to proceed with caution. Now that you have this list, use the translations of your strengths in order to help when establishing boundaries for yourself. Knowing that you have the propensity to ignore disrespect or over-work yourself in relationships not serving you, you can create safeguards for yourself that keep you from falling into these old habits.

Freedom From the Familiar ──────────

Familiarity is the muscle memory of habit. It's the mental, emotional, and physical reflex we have to what's comfortable. Familiarity will cause you to miss them, anticipate them, and have fantasies about them. Familiarity will cause you to have a full-blown fight with them in your head just because you "know" them. The job of familiarity is to maintain an open door for connection. You can't forget them, but your first challenge is to get beyond that familiarity with them.

The bond to them is broken; in order to maintain that freedom from them, you must continue maintaining the control over your environment. To do that, you have to have borders, both mentally and physically. You have to continue to guard your thoughts and your actions.

Now you may have also fasted from friends, family, and acquaintances during this time. The temporary disconnect was necessary in order to isolate yourself from potentially hazardous intruders. It kept you from conversations you weren't ready for. Fasting also kept you from being vulnerable to people you love that were being used to keep you in bondage.

Distancing yourself from people helped you to become stronger. However, you may not yet be strong enough to engage. They are still curious and some may even feel entitled to be involved in your decisions. You are not obligated to engage where you are not comfortable. If your boundaries are consistently tested or overstepped by certain people, give yourself permission to restrict their access to you. The most important thing for you right now is to control your mental and physical environment.

You will also have to come to terms with the fact that many people may not be ready to receive the new you. Don't let their opinions of your decisions or their complaints that you've changed affect you. They have no idea what you've survived through. Sometimes, moving on also means leaving people where they are until they are ready for who you are. And that's okay.

Freedom Forward Boundaries

As you walk out your freedom, there are going to be some people that are either not healthy or safe for you, not just those you have detoxed from. They don't necessarily have to be "bad" people. But if they have a negative influence over you, or if they could potentially expose you to people, places or things that you've worked hard to break free from, it may not be the best idea to allow those people in your space.

1. Make a list of people that you either need to continue to "fast" from right now (even if it's temporary) or those that you need to remain cut-off from indefinitely.

2. List any people that may require stricter boundaries as you as you move forward.

66

Sometimes, moving on also means leaving people where they are until they are ready for who you are. And that's okay.

Freedom Forward Boundaries

Now that you've created a list of people that you do not want to engage with right now, create a list of conversations you don't want to have and subjects that are off the table with other people you may encounter.

For instance, conversations with an ex that are off the table (an ex that you HAVE to talk to):

- Conversations that include nostalgia or memories of how things used to be.

- Conversations that include possibilities of rekindling your relationship.

- Conversations about them missing you.

Conversations that are off the table when other people ask you about your ex.

- How you broke up or what went wrong in the relationship.

- Them dating someone else.

Are there any other topics that you don't want to discuss with or regarding an ex? List them here.

Freedom Forward Boundaries

Are there any other topics that are off the table for family and friends? *I.e. recent life choices or decisions you've made? People you've chosen to cut off? Etc.*

Freedom Forward Boundaries

Create a list of verbal responses or actions that you will take to shut down unwanted conversations.

For instance, when a conversation with an ex takes a turn to a topic that you're not comfortable with, create some boundary statements that plainly state your position in that moment.

Boundary Statement Examples:

- That's not something I'm interested in discussing.

- We were initially talking about (topic). If you're not going to stay on the topic, then I'm hanging up.

Note: The statement has to always be about what *you* will or will not do, and not about what you want *them* to do. You can only control you, and they will likely manipulate anything you ask of them.

Create some boundary statements of your own. *In case you didn't realize, actions are "statements" as well! Be creative.*

Freedom Forward Boundaries

—————————————————— ❧ ——————————————————

When family members or friends ask you about exes, recent decisions, or other topics that you aren't comfortable with, what are some ways that you can respond to them?

Boundary Statement Examples:

- I appreciate your concern but I don't want to talk about it.

- I don't even have it in me to discuss right now, what's new with you?

- Oh, I've given that to God so I don't have to worry about it any more. How's everything on your end?

Are there any other boundary statements for for family and friends that you can t hink of? *Try to write some in your own voice.*

Being clear and setting boundaries will ensure the protection of your peace. It will alarm some people, and others will be offended. How they respond to your boundaries is not your problem. Always keep a smile and pleasant tone, but regardless of how they feel about your response, they still have to respect it. Any disrespect or persistence is your signal to distance them.

Freedom From Judgement

There are people who have seen you hit rock bottom. They've seen who you were in your past, and they may have even watched you struggle through this detox. Some may see you as a failure and define you based upon your past mistakes. As a result, they may continue to look down on you and treat you like you are broken.

You're not the only one who needed to break a habit bond. Everyone has habitual thoughts, actions, or feelings regarding others. This includes people who have always judged you. They have a habit of their negative images of you. They're comfortable with the idea that you are not enough. They have a habit of watching you fall. Don't hold that against them, but also know there is no truth in their position. Remember, you are not your mistakes. You have been forgiven and you are debt-free. If certain people cannot see that, then that's their issue, not yours. Refuse to be drawn into someone else's condemnation.

This will be easier said than done because, as humans, it is natural for us to seek validation, especially from people we've always struggled to get validation from. But when others don't validate us, we have to be self-validated. Self-validation is not an exercise in self-indulgence. It is not unhealthy self-centrism or arrogance. Self-validation is all about helping you appreciate your growth while also celebrating who you are and who you're becoming.

Self-Validation Exercise

1. What is something that you do now that you did differently when you first started this process? *Do you stop and think before making hasty decisions? Do you turn your "heart switch" off when you get overwhelmed?*

2. What is something that you know about yourself now that you didn't know before you started this process?

3. How have you changed for the better?

Self-Validation Exercise

4. What are you most grateful for today that you didn't have when you started this process?

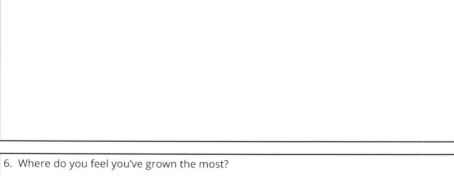

5. What are some opinions that others may have had about you before this process that aren't true today? Why are those opinions no longer true?

6. Where do you feel you've grown the most?

Support System and Accountability ———

You should have someone acting as a Personal Support System (PSS) that has supported you through this process. Going forward, we encourage you to maintain that relationship with them. In conjunction with your PSS, we highly suggest creating new local support for yourself and others. These support groups are where you can continue to get the support you need. There are several options in creating this winning circle of support.

Friends and Family ————————

Many people are blessed with friends and family that are willing to support them. Enlist those trusted friends and family members and share your journey with them. Share with them about how you felt when you started and where you are now. Invite them to celebrate what you've accomplished and to support where you're going. Ask them to help you stay accountable to your "freedom" and your healing process.

Local Small Groups ————————

Small groups are groups of like-minded people sharing a journey together. Typically, we'd find small groups in churches, but they are not exclusive to churches. In our program, any group of 12 or less is considered a small group.

With this in mind, because you've gone through the process and know what it entails, you can host a Soul-Ties Detox small group. You'd be able to help others deal with some of the same hardships of the process that you've experienced. You'll be able to hold each other accountable, lift each other up in prayer, and root for each other's success.

Virtual Support Groups

Consider joining or starting a support group. It would be like a small group but done virtually. This can be done with Zoom™, FaceTime™, Messenger™, or other similar platforms. Whatever your venue, there are ways to create small groups that extend beyond local communities. There may even be a way to connect one Soul-Ties Detox small group to another.

Your Triggers

Triggers will be a part of your norm for a while. While triggers are emotional responses to fears that we have of revisiting bad experiences, they are also reminders of what you've overcome. It will be easy to think of your triggers as reminders of your weaknesses, but you are really strong and have overcome this because you are strong. Always try to reframe your triggers into the truths of your triumph.

Use your journal to take inventory of each trigger as you come across them. Acknowledge it, write it down, and face it. When we say face it, we mean that you should be intentional about identifying why something caused a reaction and seeking to understand whether or not your trigger was a warning or a reminder.

Learning to decipher a trigger from a warning versus a reminder will do two things for you. First, it will begin to build the healthy habit of reasoning before making decisions or reacting. Secondly, you're practicing controlling yourself and your environment. When you face a trigger, you're facing an immediate emotional response. Then you're using sound reasoning to understand that response. This keeps the trigger from controlling you and giving you all of the power.

For Example:

Let's say past toxic relationships included emotional abuse through verbal assault. They cursed at you, yelled at you, pushed you in a corner, and made you feel small. This was a feeling you'll never forget and never want to experience again.

Imagine a few months have passed since you've successfully completed this program. You are in a place of mental and emotional freedom. You've begun a new friendship and you feel safe with them. One night, while out on a date, you get into a minor debate. You notice they raise their voice in excitement and it triggers you. What do you do?

First, you identify what has triggered you. In this case, it was them raising their voice. Next, you politely ask them for a time out. While you are not obligated to divulge any intimate information, you can tell them that heated debates can sometimes make you uncomfortable but that it's not them. Consider excusing yourself to go to the restroom to regain your composure. Take a few deep breaths and remind yourself that this new person is not your ex.

Anytime you meet someone new, it will be important to mentally separate new friends from the ex that sometimes still occupies space in your head. At every juncture of the relationship, you will need to evaluate who the new person is and if they are consistent.

- Are they safe for you?
- Do they exhibit characteristics that make you uncomfortable?
- How are they different from your ex?
- Are there similarities between them and your ex that you should be cognizant of?

You won't always be able to practice this in the heat of the moment, but always evaluate them and be honest about who they are as opposed to what they remind you of. This way you can make reasonable decisions about the trajectory of your relationship based on facts and observations, not feelings. This is you guarding yourself with reason rather than with triggers.

Keep Your Options Open for Emotional Support

There may be times when triggers may be too much and you suffer a deeper emotional pain. Sadness, depression, anxiety, and more can come after the kind of trauma that you suffered. If you find yourself overwhelmed, please seek help immediately. Clinical therapy can provide you with additional tools that will help facilitate further healing. This program was not designed to be a replacement for therapy.

You Are Healed Enough

We always get the question, "How do you know when you're healed?" And while there is no one-size-fits-all answer, we always respond that it's more about being "healed enough" than being totally healed. There are levels to healing. Healing happens during the time you are readjusting to your new norm.

How do you know if you're healed enough? Being healed enough doesn't mean that something doesn't hurt. It means that you've practiced managing how it affects you. You're mastering what we've already talked about in boundaries, peace, and triggers. People will disappoint you. You will make mistakes in allowing the wrong people in. So being healed enough means that you won't be as shaken the next time as you were this time.

Being healed enough means that you have a plan for when you feel like you're losing your way. You will have mastered the process of this program. You'll flush, fast, face, forgive, and move forward.

GRADUATION DAY

You are a new creature. You are different than you were over a month ago. You have a new mind, a new understanding, and a new peace. You have gained your life back, along with hope, love, and power. You can breathe again. This is your week of proclamation, celebration, and commencement.

Closing Blessing

In the name of Jesus Christ, we now commission you to:

Continue to grow. Continue to learn. Continue to cleanse
Continue to share.

Be free. Live free. Help free someone else.

—————————— ℓℓ ——————————

Praise be to the God and Father of our Lord Jesus Christ, the Father of compassion and the God of all comfort, who comforts us in all our troubles, so that we can comfort those in any trouble with the comfort we ourselves receive from God.
2 Corinthians 1:3-4 (NIV)

Made in the USA
Columbia, SC
08 January 2025

51384508R00176